BIBLE FUN-MENTIONABLES

La Lutte de Jacob by Gustave Doré (1832-1883), engraved by Charles Laplante

*A*nd Jacob remained alone, and a man wrestled with him until break of day. And when he saw that he did not prevail against Jacob, he touched the joint of Jacob's thigh, and the joint of Jacob's thigh was dislocated as he wrestled with him. And he said, "Thy name shall no more be called Jacob, but Israel, for **thou hast wrestled with God**, and with men, and hast prevailed." *Genesis 32:24-25,28*

This book is dedicated to my wife and children, to whom I am grateful
for their support and understanding, and to all who have wrestled with the Bible,
with or without suffering mysterious hip ailments.

BIBLE FUN-MENTIONABLES

A Lighthearted Look at the WILDEST Verses You've Never Been Told!

MICHAEL G. MORRIS

REVIVER

Reviver Publishing • www.reviverpublishing.com

www.biblefunmentionables.com

Bible Funmentionables contains verses from
the following public domain Bible translations:
King James Bible
Douay-Rheims Bible
Webster's Bible Translation
World English Bible
Darby Bible Translation
American Standard Version
English Revised Version
Bible in Basic English
Weymouth New Testament
and
Young's Literal Translation.

Cover design by Michael G. Morris
"The Garden of Earthly Delights" painting by Hieronymus Bosch

ISBN-13: 978-0615498256 (Reviver Publishing)
ISBN-10: 0615498256

Printed in the U.S.A.

REVIVER
Published by Reviver Publishing
www.reviverpublishing.com
info@reviverpublishing.com
First printing 2011

THE CONTENTS WHEREOF WERE THESE . . .
—1 Maccabees 15:2

THE BIBLE IN PICTURES

Choose the correct contents of this biblical illustration.

1 The two beasts of the apocalypse

2 Noah feeds the bears

3 Children mauled for ridiculing the bald

4 Early Christian martyrs being fed to wild animals

Answer: 3 (see p.65 or 2 Kings 2:23-24 for all the bears-besting-bald-bullies details!)

God brought him forth out of Egypt. He hath as it were the strength of a **unicorn.** *Numbers 24:8*

Dios lo sacó de Egipto. Tiene fuerzas como de **unicornio.**

神領他出埃及；他似乎有**野牛**之力。

Iddio che l'ha tratto d'Egitto, gli dà il vigore dell'**unicorno.**

אל מוציאם ממצרים כתועפת **ראם** לו

Бог вывел его из Египта, быстрота **единорога** у него.

Bóg wywiódł go z Egiptu, mocą **jednorożcową** był mu.

Deus eduxit illum de Aegypto cuius fortitudo similis est **rinocerotis.**

Gott hat ihn aus Ägypten geführet; seine Freudigkeit ist wie eines **Einhorns.**

Бог го изведе из Египет; Има сила, както див **вол.**

Iz Egipta Bog ga izveo, on je njemu k'o **rozi bivola.**

Le Dieu Fort qui l'a tiré d'Egypte, lui est comme les forces de la **Licorne.**

Bůh silný vyvedl je z Egypta, jako silou **jednorožcovou** byv jim.

θεός ὁ ἐξαγαγὼν αὐτοὺς ἐξ αἰγύπτου ὡς δόξα **μονοκέρωτος** αὐτῷ.

하나님이 그들을 애굽에서 인도하여 내셨으니 그 힘이 **들소와** 같도다

Bůh silný vyvedl jej z Egypta, jako udatnost **jednorožcova** jest jemu.

Gud førte det ud af Ægypten, det har en **Vildokses Horn.**

God heeft hem uit Egypte uitgevoerd; zijn krachten zijn als van een **eenhoorn.**

Gud førte ham ut av Egypten; styrke har han som en **villokse.**

Đức Chúa Trời đã dẫn người ra khỏi xứ Ê-díp-tô, Người có sức mạnh như **bò rừng.**

พระเจ้าผู้ทรงนำเขาออกมาจากอียิปต์ ทรงเป็นเสมือนพลังแห่งม้า**ยูนิคอน**

Dio, kiu elkondukis lin el Egiptujo, Estas por li kiel la forto de **bubalo.**

É Deus que os vem tirando do Egito; as suas forças são como as do **boi selvagem.**

Jumala johdatti hänen Egyptistä, hänen väkevyytensä on niinkuin **yksisarvisen** väkevyys.

Det är Gud som har fört honom ut ur Egypten. Hans styrka är såsom en **vildoxes.**

Tanrı onları Mısırdan çıkardı, Onun **yaban öküzü** gibi gücü var.

Na Ihowa ratou i whakaputa mai i Ihipa; kei te te **unikanga** tona kaha.

Ấy là Đức Chúa Trời đã rút dân đó ra khỏi xứ Ê-díp-tô; Chúng có sức mạnh như **bò rừng** vậy.

INTRODUCTION

"IN THE BEGINNING . . ."

*A*re there really parts of the Bible that your teachers and preachers <u>don't</u> want you to know?

It turns out that the most widely read book of all time may also be the most *selectively* read book of all time. It's so big that we usually just find the information we need and ignore the rest—like the yellow pages, but with fewer mechanics and a lot more bloodshed. In fact, your own preacher may not even know some of these verses exist. Equally likely, they are the verses that were secretly passed around at Bible college, never to be spoken again.

The religiously incorrect passages are just cringe-worthy enough to avoid preaching, because they would shock parents, titillate teens, and/or scar small children, basically requiring too much sermon time to try to explain away.

So how do you know if you've ever heard these unspoken scriptures? See how many answers come to mind in the following pop quiz:

- What must you never do to the corners of your beard?
- Can the faithful drink poison and live?
- What are the necessary ingredients for making dragon explosives?
- Which is an abomination to eat: the ostrich or the locust?
- Are you better off living with a wicked woman or with a lion and a dragon?
- Does God like your tattoo?
- God gives Satan permission to ruin whose life?
- Yahweh promises to give starving complainers meat until it comes out of their what?
- Who died by both hanging and spontaneous combustion?
- After God spoke to the fish, what did it vomit out?
- If you dig a hole and an ass falls in it, are you responsible for your inconsiderate ass's hole?
- What did the Pharisees do with mint, dill, and cumin that bothered Jesus so much?
- Why did Samson disrobe 30 men?
- Why did Jesus kill a fig tree?

These questions all come from the Bible's D-list: all the verses that preachers **D**on't like, **D**on't preach, and **D**on't want you to know about—and they're also some of the most entertaining, eye-popping, and enlightening! The surprising and sometimes shocking quotes can actually impart insights into the Bible and the people who wrote it, while also providing what some scholars call a "biblical chucklefest."

If you thought that the Bible was just a bunch of boring old stories, you'd be only seven eighths right. You've already heard the pleasant and inoffensive Bible, so now discover the whole truth as you explore *Bible Funmentionables*.

Pop Quiz Answers: mutilate; yes; pitch, fat, and hair; ostrich; lion and dragon; no; Job; nostrils; Judas; Jonah; yes; tithe; to pay off a bet; it was fruitless.

BIZARRE
OLD TESTAMENT

Through no fault of their own, the authors of the Bible lived a long, long time ago—before the invention of the wheelbarrow, before crossbows, and before the era of fact-checking. They wrote for a people who demanded excitement in their stories: talking animals, talking ghosts, and countless people who let their fists do the talking. Luckily for Bible Funmentionable lovers everywhere, these authors were never commanded "thou shalt not exaggerate to make a point."

The Lord God said, "It is not good that the man should be alone. **I will make him a helper** suitable for him." Out of the ground the Lord God formed every animal of the field and every bird of the sky, and brought them to the man to see what he would call them. Whatever the man called every living creature, that was its name. The man gave names to all livestock, and to the birds of the sky, and to every animal of the field, but for man there was not found a helper suitable for him.

Genesis 2:18-20 ⛏ *Thank you, Adam, for not settling for any of those wild animals as companions and instead telling God, "Let's try something a little more human and maybe feminine this time."*

And after that, men began to be multiplied upon the earth, and daughters were born to them. **The sons of God seeing the daughters of men**, that they were fair, took themselves wives of all which they chose.

Genesis 6:1-2 ⛏ *But which set of parents did they spend the holidays with?*

The Nephilim were on the earth in those days, and also after that, **when God's sons came to men's daughters**, who gave birth to their children. They were the mighty heroes of old, the famous men.

Genesis 6:4 ⛏ *Gods having mighty, heroic offspring with humans? It sounds almost mythological.*

And the ass said to Balaam, "Am I not your ass upon which you have ridden all your life unto this day? And have I ever done this to you before?" Balaam said, "No."

Numbers 22:30 ⛏ *Known as "The Mr. Ed Miracle", the Lord talks out of his—that is, by means of his donkey.*

And now slay every male, even of the children, and put to death the women that have carnally known men. But the girls and **all the women that are virgins save for yourselves**.

Numbers 31:17-18 ⛏ *Now that's how you wage war old school.*

UNSAFE PASSAGE
Unsuitable for
Student-Led Prayer

And Jehovah said unto Moses, "When thou goest back into Egypt, see that thou do before Pharaoh all the wonders which I have put in thy hand, **but I will harden his heart and he will not let the people go**. And thou shalt say unto Pharaoh, 'Thus saith Jehovah, "Israel is my son, my first-born, and I have said unto thee, 'Let my son go, that he may serve me,' and thou hast refused to let him go. Behold, I will slay thy son, thy first-born."'"
Exodus 4:21-23

THE UNTOLD STORY
The Deleted Details from Popular Passages

But **Jehovah hardened Pharaoh's heart**, and he did not let the children of Israel go.
Exodus 10:20

But **Jehovah hardened Pharaoh's heart**, and he would not let them go.
Exodus 10:27

And **all the first-born in the land of Egypt shall die**, from the first-born of Pharaoh that sitteth upon his throne, even unto the first-born of the maid-servant that is behind the mill, and all the first-born of cattle.
Exodus 11:5 📖 *Sounds like Pharaoh was willing to let the Israelites go, but God seems to have had some plagues he still wanted to show off. Because really, what's the point of having such awesome plagues if you never use them?*

Through all these 40 years **your clothing did not get old** or your feet become tired.
Deuteronomy 8:4 📖 *That's why they wandered in the desert so long; they were testing their magical clothes.*

BIBLE FUNMENTIONABLE! QUIZ

SHALT THOU OR SHALT THOU NOT?

📖 Pulpits and religious airwaves are often full of "Thou Shalt Nots", but how much of that is a true reflection of the <u>explicit</u> DO's and DON'Ts of the Bible, and how much is subject to interpretation? Categorize the following as **FORBIDDEN, ALLOWED,** or **NOT MENTIONED.**

1 Women Speaking In Church
2 War Crimes
3 Cock Fighting
4 Abortion
5 Men with Long Hair
6 Beating Your Servant
7 Polygamy

8 Drinking to Forget Your Troubles
9 A Widow Not Marrying Her Brother-in-law
10 Universal Public Education
11 Ignoring the Poor & Homeless
12 Slavery
13 Smoking

14 Democracy
15 Ethnic Cleansing
16 Human Cloning
17 Eating Rock Badgers
18 Female Teachers
19 Not Observing the Sabbath
20 Praying in Public

1 Forbidden (1 Cor 14:34); 2 Allowed (1 Sm 15:3); 3 Not Mentioned; 4 Not Mentioned; 5 Forbidden (1 Cor 11:14); 6 Allowed (Ex 21:21); 7 Allowed (1 Kgs 11:3); 8 Allowed (Prov 31:7); 9 Forbidden (Deut 25:5); 10 Not Mentioned; 11 Forbidden (Matt 25:41-43); 12 Allowed (Lev 25:44); 13 Not Mentioned; 14 Not Mentioned; 15 Allowed (Num 33:55); 16 Not Mentioned; 17 Forbidden (Lev 11:5); 18 Forbidden (1Tim 2:12); 19 Forbidden and Allowed (Ex 31:14 and Col 2:16); 20 Forbidden (Matt 6:5-6)

Passage of Questionable Relevance

When thou goest forth to battle against thine enemies, and Jehovah thy God delivereth them into thy hands, and thou carriest them away captive, and seest among the captives a beautiful woman, and thou hast a desire unto her, and wouldest take her to thee to wife, then thou shalt bring her home to thy house. And she shall shave her head, and pare her nails, and she shall put the raiment of her captivity from off her, and shall remain in thy house and bewail her father and her mother a full month. And after that thou shalt go in unto her and be her husband, and she shall be thy wife. And it shall be, **if thou have no delight in her**, then thou shalt let her go whither she will, but thou shalt not sell her at all for money. Thou shalt not deal with her as a slave, because thou hast humbled her.

Deuteronomy 21:10-14 📖 In ancient Israel, "Take my wife, please!" was less of a punch line and more of an ultra-quickie divorce proceeding.

TOP TEN
The Best of the Worst

If two men are fighting, and the wife of one of them, coming to the help of her husband, **takes the other by the private parts**, her hand is to be cut off. Have no pity on her.
Deuteronomy 25:11-12 📖 A good wife is always willing to lend a hand to a husband in need.

The trees went forth on a time to anoint a king over them, and they said to the olive tree, "Reign thou over us." But the olive tree said to them, "Should I leave my fatness, with which by me they honor God and man, and go to be promoted over the trees?" And the trees said to the fig tree, "Come thou, and reign over us." But the fig tree said to them, "Should I forsake my sweetness and my good fruit and go to be promoted over the trees?" Then said the trees to the vine, "Come thou, and reign over us." And the vine said to them, "Should I leave **my wine, which cheereth God** and man, and go to be promoted over the trees?"

Then said all the trees to the bramble, "Come thou, and reign over us." And the bramble said to the trees, "If in truth ye anoint me king over you, then come and put your trust in my shadow. And if not, let fire come out of the bramble and devour the cedars of Lebanon."

Judges 9:8-15 📖 How "cheerful" must God have been when he created the platypus, star-nosed mole, angora rabbit, blobfish, and proboscis monkey?

LIFE BEFORE BLUEPRINTS
Ezekiel 40-43

📖 Instead of revealing concrete solutions to famine, war, disease, etc., for some reason the Bible goes into mind-numbing detail on how to build a temple. Do not operate heavy machinery while reading!

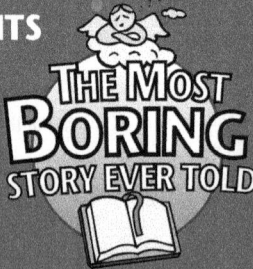

THE MOST BORING STORY EVER TOLD

Under arson threat, riddle answer revealed

To pay off wager, Samson attacks 30

TIMNAH, Sorek Valley - And Samson said, "Let me propose a riddle to you. If you are able to give me the answer before the seven days of the feast are over, I will give you thirty linen robes and thirty changes of clothing. But if you are not able to give me the answer, then you will have to give me thirty linen robes and thirty changes of clothing." And they said to him, "Put forth your riddle and let us see what it is." And he said, "*Out of the taker of food came food, and out of the strong came the sweet.*" And at the end of three days they were still not able to give the answer. So on the fourth day they said to Samson's wife, "Get from your husband the answer to his question by some trick or other, or we will have you and your father's house burned with fire. Did you get us here to take all we have?" Then Samson's wife, weeping over him, said, "Truly you have no love for me but only hate. You have put a hard question to the children of my people and have not given me the answer." And he said to her, "See, I have not given the answer even to my father or my mother. Am I to give it to you?" And all the seven days of the feast she went on weeping over him, and on the seventh day he gave her the answer, because she gave him no peace, and she sent word of it to the children of her people. Then on the seventh day, before he went into the bride's room, the men of the town said to him, "What is sweeter than honey? And what is stronger than a lion?" And he said to them, "If you had not plowed with my heifer, you would not have gotten the answer to my riddle." And the spirit of the Lord came rushing on him, and he went down to Ashkelon and, attacking thirty men there, took their clothing from them and gave it to the men who had given the answer to his hard question. Then, full of wrath, he went back to his father's house.

Judges 14:12-19 ☟ There are three obvious lessons here: 1. If you can't figure out someone's riddle, threaten them with arson. 2. To pay off a bet, beating up 30 men and stealing their robes is always an option. 3. Know how many men you can safely assault before making your wager.

And he found a fresh jawbone of an ass, and put forth his hand, and took it, and smote a thousand men therewith.

Judges 15:15 ☟ Make sure the ass jawbone is fresh!

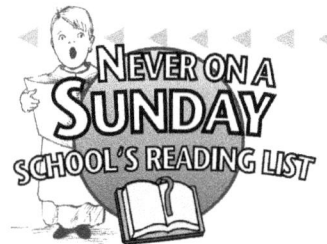

NEVER ON A SUNDAY SCHOOL'S READING LIST

And Saul said to his servants, "*Seek me a woman that hath a divining spirit*, and I will go to her and inquire by her." And his servants said to him, "There is a woman that hath a divining spirit at Endor."

1 Samuel 28:7 ☟ Anyone with divining spirits are to be stoned to death (see Leviticus 20:27), but they are evidently good enough for Saul. They are also successful in speaking to the irritated ghost of Samuel who lets Saul know that he didn't appreciate being disturbed from the grave—oh and that Saul will be dead within 24 hours. (see 1 Samuel 28:15-20).

And I will destroy all the house of Achab, and I will cut off from Achab him that pisseth against the wall, and him that is shut up, and the meanest in Israel.

2 Kings 9:8

Bible Funmentionables Poster Series

But as one was felling a beam, ***the axe head fell into the water***, and he cried and said, "Alas, master!" for it was borrowed. And the man of God said, "Where fell it?" And he showed him the place. And he cut down a stick and cast it in thither, and the iron floated.

2 Kings 6:5-6 📖 *Floating Axe Heads: my new band name!*

And there was a great famine in Samaria, and so long did the siege continue, till ***the head of an ass was sold for fourscore pieces of silver***, and the fourth part of a cabe of pigeon's dung for five pieces of silver.

2 Kings 6:25 📖 *"Yeah, I'll take…um…three ass heads and half a cabe of pigeon dung."*

As they were burying a man, they saw a band of men coming, and they cast the body into the sepulchre of Elisha. And when it had touched ***the bones of Elisha***, he revived and stood up on his feet.

2 Kings 13:21 📖 *Anthropologists note that ancient Israel had the highest resurrection rate in the world.*

But Rabshakeh said to them, "Has my master sent me to your master, and to you, to speak these words? Hasn't he sent me to the men who sit on the wall, that ***they may eat their own dung*** and drink their own urine with you?"

2 Kings 18:27 📖 *Rabshakeh certainly had a way with words.*

2 KINGS 18:27 — Eat Dung! — UNLIKELY SIGN — From a Fan in the Stands

The Bible in Headlines

God approves of angel's plan to lie

JERUSALEM, Judea - And Micaiah said, "Therefore hear ye the word of Jehovah: I saw Jehovah sitting upon his throne, and all the host of heaven standing on his right hand and on his left. And Jehovah said, 'Who shall entice Ahab king of Israel, that he may go up and fall at Ramoth-gilead?' And one spake saying after this manner, and another saying after that manner. And there came forth a spirit, and stood before Jehovah, and said, 'I will entice him.' And Jehovah said unto him, 'Wherewith?' And he said, '***I will go forth and will be a lying spirit*** in the mouth of all his prophets.' And he said, 'Thou shalt entice him and shalt prevail also. Go forth, and do so.'"

2 Chronicles 18:18-21 📖 *God apparently approves of lying for the right reasons.*

Behold, Yahweh will strike with a great plague your people, and your children, and your wives, and all your substance, and you shall have **great sickness by disease of your bowels**, until your bowels fall out by reason of the sickness, day by day.

2 Chronicles 21:14-15 *I think I'd prefer a good, old-fashioned locust plague.*

And as he was sleeping, **hot dung out of a swallow's nest** fell upon his eyes, and he was made blind.

Tobit 2:11 *"Now I lay me down to sleep, I pray the Lord my eyes to keep free of hot swallow's dung."*

It is not right for a woman to be dressed in man's clothing, or for a man to put on a woman's robe. Whoever does such things is disgusting to the Lord your God.

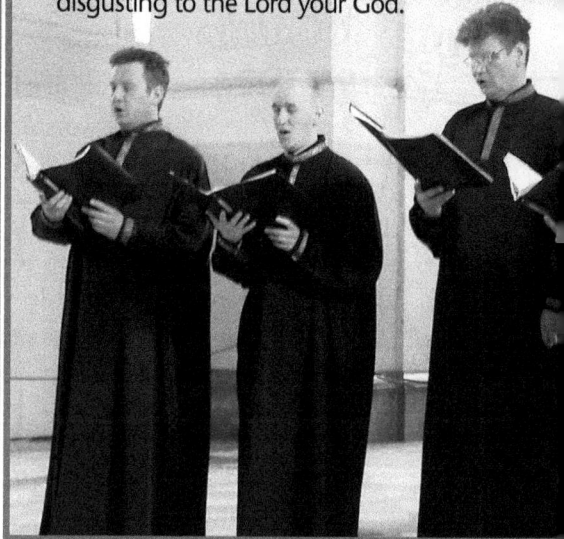

Deuteronomy 22:5   *Bible Funmentionables Poster Series*

UNSAFE PASSAGE
Unsuitable for Student-Led Prayer

Now it happened on the same day that Sara, daughter of Raguel, in Rages a city of the Medes, received a reproach from one of her father's servant maids, because she had been given to seven husbands, and **a devil named Asmodeus had killed them** at their first going in unto her.

Tobit 3:7-8 *"Honey, what was that about a devil having killed your six previous husbands?" "Go in unto that, darling, it's our honeymoon!"*

And she struck twice upon his neck, and cut off his head, and took off his canopy from the pillars, and rolled away his headless body. And after a while she went out, and delivered the head of Holofernes to her maid, and **bade her put it into her wallet**.

Judith 13:10-11 *A good maid hides the family's secrets.*

His breasts are full of milk, and his bones are moistened with marrow.

Job 21:24 *It's a bit strange that this is a description of a guy we are supposed to envy because of his comfortable life. Never tried it myself, but it sounds rather un-comfortable.*

If I beheld the sun when it shined and the moon going in brightness, and my heart in secret hath rejoiced, and I have kissed my hand with my mouth, **this also would be a very great iniquity**, and a denial against the most high God.

Job 31:26-28 *Kissing your own hand has dropped off the charts of the Top 40 Sins.*

Passage of Questionable Relevance

Those who have no fear of God keep wrath stored up in their hearts. They give no cry for help when they are made prisoners. They come to their end while they are still young. Their life is short like that of **those who are used for sex purposes** in the worship of their gods.

Job 36:13-14 ☄ Unique among best-selling books, not a single editor is credited in the Bible. Surely a sharp editor would have trimmed the last line to "Their life is short."

Turn to me, O Lord, and deliver my soul. O save me for thy mercy's sake, for there is no one in death that is mindful of thee, and **who shall confess to thee in hell?**

Psalms 6:4-5 ☄ Translation: Save my life, or I won't pray to you anymore.

Behold, **they belch out with their mouth**. Swords are in their lips. "For who," say they, "doth hear us?" But thou, O Lord, shalt laugh at them. Thou shalt have all the heathen in derision.

Psalms 59:7-8 ☄ Did some ancients have other ways of belching besides using their mouths?

The slothful **hideth his hand under his armpit**, and will not so much as bring it to his mouth.

Proverbs 19:24 ☄ They just don't make the slothful like they used to.

WHOLLY UNHOLY The Dark Side of the Bible

Their infants also shall be dashed in pieces before their eyes. Their houses shall be rifled, and their wives ravished. And their bows shall dash the young men in pieces, and they shall have no pity on the fruit of the womb. Their eye shall not spare children. But wild beasts of the desert shall lie there, and their houses shall be full of doleful creatures. And ostriches shall dwell there, and wild goats shall dance there. And wolves shall cry in their castles, and jackals in the pleasant palaces. And her time is near to come, and her days shall not be prolonged.

Isaiah 13:16,18,21-22 ☄ Ostriches taking over all the houses, wolves in castles, dancing goats—makes you kind of forget all those dead infants and fetuses.

*A*nd he that strongly squeezeth the papa to bring out milk, straineth out butter. And he that violently bloweth his nose, bringeth out blood. And he that provoketh wrath, bringeth forth strife.

Proverbs 30:33   Bible Funmentionables Poster Series

He that winketh with the eye shall cause sorrow, and the foolish in lips shall be beaten.

Proverbs 10:10   *Bible Funmentionables Poster Series*

Because he did not put me to death before my birth took place, so my mother's body would have been my last resting-place, and she would have been with child forever. Why did I come from my mother's body to see pain and sorrow, so that my days might be wasted with shame?

> *Jeremiah 20:17-18* ⚱ *Lamenting the fact that you weren't aborted is a sure sign that it's time to seek professional help.*

Make him drunk, because he lifted up himself against the Lord. And Moab shall **dash his hand in his own vomit**, and he also shall be in derision.

> *Jeremiah 48:26* ⚱ *Sounds like Moab had a drinking and a hand-dashing problem.*

Her filthiness was in her skirts. She didn't remember her latter end. Therefore is she come down wonderfully. She has no comforter. See, Yahweh, my affliction, for the enemy has magnified himself.

> *Lamentations 1:9* ⚱ *Cleanliness is next to godliness. Filthiness, on the other hand, is apparently something you really don't want in your skirts.*

And he said to me, "Son of man, eat all that thou shalt find. **Eat this book**, and go speak to the children of Israel." And I opened my mouth, and he caused me to eat that book. And he said to me, "Son of man, thy belly shall eat, and thy bowels shall be filled with this book which I give thee." And I did eat it, and it was sweet as honey in my mouth.

> *Ezekiel 3:1-3* ⚱ *"Now that was a good book."*

And I will sell your sons and your daughters by the hands of the children of Juda, and they shall sell them to the Sabeans, a nation far off, for the Lord hath spoken it.

> *Joel 3:8* ⚱ *Good thinking to have a buyer all lined up before you make a threat like that.*

The Lord stood upon a wall made by a plumbline, with a plumbline in his hand. And the Lord said unto me, "Amos, what seest thou?" And I said, "**A plumbline**."

> *Amos 7:7-8* ⚱ *Still unanswered is what other tools God keeps on hand. You can't have made all of creation without a tape measure, a cordless drill, and hopefully he splurged on a quality nail gun.*

BIZARRE

NEW TESTAMENT

Compared to the Old Testament, the New Testament has fewer arcane laws, animal sacrifices, and epic battles, but the odd pronouncements still abound. Just remember, as it says in some book somewhere, "seek and ye shall find."

When he came to the other side, into the country of the Gergesenes, two people possessed with demons met him there, coming forth out of the tombs, exceedingly fierce, so that no man could pass by that way. Behold, they cried out, saying, "What do we have to do with you, Jesus, Son of God? Have you come here to torment us before the time?" Now there was a herd of many pigs feeding far away from them. The demons begged him, saying, "If you cast us out, permit us to go away into the herd of pigs." He said to them, "Go!" They came out, and went into the herd of pigs, and behold, **the whole herd of pigs rushed down the cliff** into the sea, and died in the water.

Matthew 8:28-32 — *Just like a magician who rips up an audience member's $20 bill and later returns it to them in mint condition, we can only hope that the pig herder got his demon-free, resuscitated pigs back.*

THE UNTOLD STORY
The Deleted Details from Popular Passages

Now, while they were going, some of the watchmen came into the town and gave news to the chief priests of all the things which had taken place. And when they had come together with those in authority, and had made their decision, they gave much money to the watchmen, saying, "**Say that his disciples came by night and took him away secretly** while we were sleeping. And if this comes to the ruler's ears, we will see that he does not make you responsible." So they took the money, and did as they had been ordered, and this account has been current among the Jews till the present time.

Matthew 28:11-15 — *Matthew <u>really</u> doesn't want you to fall for a popular belief at the time—that the disciples secretly removed Jesus' body from the tomb! To combat such rumors, Matthew conveniently reports that the guards were bribed to claim that the disciples did just that. So that explains that silly rumor.*

*T*hen his disciples, leaving him, all fled away. And a certain young man followed him, having a linen cloth cast about his naked body, and they laid hold on him. But he, casting off the linen cloth, fled from them naked.

Mark 14:51

BIBLE FUNMENTIONABLE QUIZ

"THE SCRIPTURE SAITH IN VAIN"

The New Testament authors were so eager to show Jesus fulfilling ancient prophecies that some of their references miss the mark. Match the New Testament reference to its actual location.

1 And he came and dwelt in a city called Nazareth, that it might be fulfilled which was **spoken by the prophets**, "He shall be called a Nazarene." *Matthew 2:23*

2 Then was fulfilled that which was spoken by **Jeremiah** the prophet, saying, "And they took the thirty pieces of silver, the price of him that was priced, whom certain of the children of Israel did price." *Matthew 27:9*

3 Even as it is said in the **book of Isaiah** the prophet, "See, I send my servant before your face, who will make ready your way." *Mark 1:2*

4 He that believes on me, as **the scripture has said**, "Out of his belly shall flow rivers of living water." *John 7:38*

5 Do ye think that **the scripture saith** in vain, "The spirit that dwelleth in us lusteth to envy"? *James 4:5*

A Not in the Bible

B Malachi 3:1

C Not in the Bible

D Zechariah 11:12

E Not in the Bible

Answers: 1-A, 2-D, 3-B, 4-C, 5-E. Also acceptable are 1-C, 1-E, 4-A, 4-E, 5-A, and 5-C.

And Jesus came to them and said, "All authority has been given to me in heaven and on earth. Go then, and make disciples of all the nations, giving them baptism in the name of the Father and of the Son and of the Holy Spirit, teaching them to keep all the rules which I have given you. And see, **I am ever with you**, even to the end of the world."

Matthew 28:18-20 ☙ *Then what? Well, nothing. This gospel story ends right there. No ascension, which would have been a noteworthy event, no walking off into the sunset, no retiring to the coast of France. Some authors struggle with endings, but we're talking critical plot resolution here.*

THE UNTOLD STORY
The Deleted Details from Popular Passages

Behold, I have given you authority to **tread upon serpents** and scorpions, and over all the power of the enemy, and nothing shall by any means hurt you.

Luke 10:19 ☙ *Join the Church of the Scorpion Tramplers today!*

Herod and his soldiers humiliated him and mocked him. Dressing him in luxurious clothing, they sent him back to Pilate. **Herod and Pilate became friends** with each other that very day, for before that they were enemies with each other.

Luke 23:11-12 ☙ *Experiencing trying times together can make for some of the most lasting friendships.*

Then Jesus said to them, "Truly I say to you, if you do not **take the flesh of the Son of man for food**, and if you do not take his blood for drink, you have no life in you. He who takes my flesh for food and my blood for drink has eternal life, and I will take him up from the dead at the last day. My flesh is true food and my blood is true drink. He who takes my flesh for food and my blood for drink is in me and I in him. As the living Father has sent me, and I have life because of the Father, even so he who takes me for his food will have life because of me. This is the bread which has come down from heaven. It is not like the food which your fathers had. They took of the manna and are dead, but he who takes this bread for food will have life forever." Jesus said these things in the Synagogue while he was teaching at Capernaum. Then, hearing this, a number of his disciples said, "This is a hard saying. Who is able to take in such teaching?" When Jesus became conscious that **his disciples were protesting about what he said**, he said to them, "Does this give you trouble?"

John 6:53-61 ☙ *Jesus, ixnay on the annibalismcay.*

And Peter opened his mouth and said, "Of a truth, I perceive that God is **no respecter of persons**."

Acts 10:34 📖 *This is an unfortunate turn of phrase which is actually attempting to express the idea that God is not showing favoritism.*

With the knowledge that **the law is made, not for the upright man**, but for those who have no respect for law and order, for evil men and sinners, for the unholy and those who have no religion, for those who put their fathers or mothers to death, for takers of life.

1 Timothy 1:9 📖 *The Bible offers you a clear choice: you can either be upright or you can be a sociopathic, patricidal atheist.*

THE UNTOLD STORY
The Deleted Details from Popular Passages

The bishop therefore must be without reproach, **the husband of one wife**, temperate, sober-minded, orderly, given to hospitality, apt to teach. Let deacons be husbands of one wife, ruling their children and their own houses well.

1 Timothy 3:2,12 📖 *I understand the early church's concern about polygamist bishops. Imagine having to keep more than one wife silent in church.*

But the Spirit says clearly that in later times some will be turned away from the faith, giving their minds to spirits of deceit and the teachings of evil spirits, through the false ways of men whose words are untrue, whose hearts are burned as with a heated iron, **who keep men from being married** and from taking food which God made to be taken with praise by those who have faith and true knowledge.

1 Timothy 4:1-3 📖 *Bachelors: avoiding commitment or under evil spirits?*

Elijah was a man of flesh and blood as we are, and he made a strong prayer that there might be no rain, and there was **no rain on the earth for three years and six months**.

James 5:17 📖 *Of course, there must have been thousands of people desperately praying for rain whose prayers went unanswered. But that's why God gets paid the big bucks: picking sides on competing prayers.*

Jesus said unto them, "If you fast, you will beget sin upon yourselves. **If you pray**, you'll be condemned. If you give to charity, you will cause harm unto your souls."

Gospel of Thomas #14 📖 *Exhibit A of why the Gospel of Thomas might have bothered the early church leaders.*

ANGRY GOD

These days God seems to have it all: worldwide name recognition, a multitude of followers, and his name invoked at the end of most prayers and sneezes. But this was not always the case. In the early days of his career, Jehovah was just another god fighting for market share in a region saturated with highly attractive gods. Over 20 different gods are mentioned by name in about 175 places in the Bible, and like the wicked queen in Snow White, *when God got dissed, God got mad.*

Then Judah said to Onan, **"Sleep with your brother's wife** and fulfill your duty to her as a brother-in-law to raise up offspring for your brother." But Onan knew that the child would not be his, so whenever he slept with his brother's wife, he spilled his semen on the ground to keep from providing offspring for his brother. What he did was wicked in the Lord's sight, so he put him to death also.

> *Genesis 38:8-10* 📖 *God takes a very bold stance with his pro-brother-in-law-impregnating-his-widowed-sister-in-law policy. Don't think he's not watching, men!*

And be ready against the third day, for on the third day **Jehovah will come down in the sight of all the people** upon Mount Sinai. And thou shalt set bounds unto the people round about, saying, "Take heed to yourselves, that ye go not up into the mount or touch the border of it. Whosoever toucheth the mount shall be surely put to death. No hand shall touch him, but he shall surely be stoned or shot through. Whether it be beast or man, he shall not live. When the trumpet soundeth long, they shall come up to the mount."

> *Exodus 19:11-13* 📖 *And the Lord said, "Shoot the animals that touch the mountain!" Hey, it's not like they weren't warned.*

He said to them, "Thus says Yahweh, the God of Israel, 'Every man put his sword on his thigh, and go back and forth from gate to gate throughout the camp, and **every man kill his brother**, and every man his companion, and every man his neighbor.'" The sons of Levi did according to the word of Moses, and there fell of the people that day about three thousand men.

> *Exodus 32:27-28* 📖 *In today's secular society, the "God told me to kill" defense is lamentably unpersuasive.*

TOP TEN
The Best of the Worst

"GOD HATH STOOD IN THE CONGREGATION OF GODS" (Ps. 82:1)

📖 Did God believe that other gods actually existed—gods that no living human currently believes in? The Bible clearly makes it sound that way. Here are the Bible's most popular lowercase 'g' gods.

God	Times Cited	God	Times Cited
Baal	61	Baalzebub	4
Asherah	40	Adrammelech	3
Baalim	18	Ashtoreth	3
Dagon	12	Milcom	3
Chemosh	8	Bel	2
Molech	7	Jupiter	2
Baalpeor	6	Nisroch	2

But if you do not give ear to the voice of **The Lord your God**, and take care to do all his orders and his laws which I give you today, then all these **curses** will come on you and overtake you. You will be cursed in the town **a**nd cursed in the field. A **curse** will be on your basket and on your bread-basin. A curse will be on the fruit of your body, and on the fruit of your land, on the increase of your cattle, and the young of your flock. You will be cursed when you come in and cursed when you go out. The Lord will send on you cursing and trouble and punishment in everything to which you put your hand, till sudden destruction overtakes you, because of your evil ways in which you have been false to me. The Lord will send disease after disease on you, till you have been cut off by death from the land to which you are going. The Lord will send wasting disease, and burning pain, and flaming heat against you, keeping back the rain till your land is waste and dead. So will it be till your destruction is complete. And the heaven over your heads will be brass, and the earth under you hard as iron. The Lord will make the rain of your land powder and dust, sending it down on you from heaven till your destruction is complete. The Lord will let you be overcome by your haters. You will go out against them one way, and you will go in flight before them seven ways. You will be the cause of fear among all the kingdoms of the earth. Your bodies will be meat for all the birds of the air and the beasts of the earth. There will be no one to send them away. The Lord will send on you the disease of Egypt, and other sorts of skin diseases which nothing will make well. He will make your minds diseased, and your eyes blind, and your hearts wasted with fear. You will go feeling your way when the sun is high, **like** a blind man for whom all is dark, and nothing will go well for you: you will be crushed and made poor forever, and you will have **no** savior. You will take a wife, but an **other** man will have the use of her. The house which your hands have made will never be your resting-place. You will make a vine-garden, and never take the fruit of it. Your ox will be put to death before your eyes, but its flesh will not be your food. Your ass will be violently taken away before your face, and will not be given back to you. Your sheep will be given to your haters, and there will be no savior for you. Your sons and your daughters will be given to another people, and your eyes will be wasted away with looking and weeping for them all the day, and you will have no power to do anything. The fruit of your land and all the work of your hands will be food for a nation which is strange to you and to your fathers. You will only be crushed down and kept under forever, so that the things which your eyes have to see will send you out of your minds. The Lord will send a skin disease, attacking your knees and your legs, bursting out from your feet to the top of your head, so that nothing will make you well. And you, and the king whom you have put over you, will the Lord take away to a nation strange to you and to your fathers. There you will be servants to other **god**s of wood and stone. And you will become a wonder and a name of shame among all the nations where the Lord will take you. You will take much seed out into the field, and get little in, for the locust will get it. You will put in vines and take care of them, but you will get no wine or grapes from them, for they will be food for worms. Your land will be full of olive trees, but there will be no oil for the comfort of your body, for your olive tree will give no fruit. You will have sons and daughters, but they will not be yours, for they will go away prisoners into a strange land. All your trees and the fruit of your land will be the locust's. The man from a strange land who is living among you will be lifted up higher and higher over you, while you go down lower and lower. He will let you have his wealth at interest, and will have no need of yours. He will be the head and you the tail. And all these **curses** will come after you and overtake you, till your destruction is complete, because you did not give ear to the voice of the Lord your God, or keep his laws and his orders which he gave you. These things will come on you and on your seed, to be a sign and a wonder forever, because you did not give honor to the Lord your God, worshipping him gladly, with joy in your hearts on account of all your wealth of good things. For this cause you will become servants to those whom the Lord your God will send against you, without food and drink and clothing, and in need of all things, and he will put a yoke of iron on your neck till he has put an end to you. The Lord will send a nation against you from the farthest ends of the earth, coming with the flight of an eagle, a nation whose language is strange to you, a hard-faced nation, who will have no respect for the old or mercy for the young. He will take the fruit of your cattle and of your land till death puts an end to you. He will let you have nothing of your grain or wine or oil or any of the increase of your cattle or the young of your flock, till he has made your destruction complete. Your towns will be shut in by his armies, till your high walls, in which you put your faith, have come down. His armies will be round your towns, through all your land which the Lord your God has given you. And your food will be the fruit of your body, the flesh of the sons and daughters which the Lord your God has given you, because of your bitter need and the cruel grip of your haters. That man among you who is soft and used to comfort will be hard and cruel to his brother, and to his dear wife, and to his children who are still living, and will not give to any of them the flesh of his children which will be his food because he has no other, in the cruel grip of your haters on all your towns. The most soft and delicate of your women, who would not **so** much as put her foot on the earth, so delicate is she, will be hard-hearted to her husband and to her son and to her daughter, and to her baby newly come to birth, and to the children of her body, for having no other food, she will make a meal of them secretly, because of her bitter need and the cruel grip of your haters on all your towns. If you will not take care to **do** all the words of this law, recorded in this book, honoring that name of glory and of fear, the Lord your God, then the Lord your God will make your punishment, and the punishment of your seed, a thing to be wondered at, great punishments and cruel diseases stretching on through long years. He will send on you again all the dise**as**es of Egypt, which were a cause of fear to you, and they will take you in their grip. And all the diseases and the pains not recorded in the book of this law will the Lord send on you till your destruction is complete. And you will become a very small band, though your numbers were like the stars of heaven, because you did not give ear to the voice of the Lord your God. And as the Lord took delight in doing you good and increasing you, so the Lord will take pleasure in cutting you off and causing your destruction, and you will be uprooted from the land which you are about to take as your heritage. And **the Lord** will send you wandering among all peoples, from one end of the earth to the other. There you will be servants to other gods, of wood and stone, gods of which you and your fathers had no knowledge. And even among these nations there will be no peace for you, and no rest for your feet. But the Lord will give you there a shaking heart and wasting eyes and weariness of soul. Your very life will be hanging in doubt before you, and day and night will be dark with fears, and nothing in life will be certain. In the morning you will say, "If only it was evening!" And at evening you will say, "If only morning would come!" because of the fear in your hearts and the things which your eyes will see. And the Lord will take you back to Egypt again in ships, by the way of which I **said** to you. You will never see it again. There you will be offering yourselves as men-servants and women-servants to your haters for a price, and no man will take you.

Deuteronomy 28:15-68

And Miriam and Aaron spoke against Moses because of **the Ethiopian woman whom he had married**, for he had married an Ethiopian woman. And the Lord came down in the pillar of the cloud, and stood in the door of the tabernacle, and called Aaron and Miriam, and they both came forth. And the anger of the Lord was kindled against them, and he departed. And the cloud departed from off the tabernacle, and behold, Miriam became leprous, white as snow. And Aaron looked upon Miriam, and behold, she was leprous.

Numbers 12:1,5,9,10 ⚅ In an inspired ironic twist, Miriam complains about Moses' marrying a black woman and she gets turned pure white. The part about punishing Miriam and not Aaron is less ironic and more biblically predictable.

And after the people had been numbered, David's heart was troubled. And David said to the Lord, "Great has been my sin in doing this, but now, O Lord, be pleased to take away the sin of your servant, for I have done very foolishly." And David got up in the morning. Now the word of the Lord had come to the prophet Gad, David's seer, saying, "Go and say to David, 'The Lord says, "**Three things are offered to you**. Say which of them you will have, and I will do it to you."'" So Gad came to David, and gave him word of this and said to him, "Are there to be three years when there is not enough food in your land? or will you go in flight from your haters for three months while they go after you? or will you have three days of violent disease in your land? Take thought and say what answer I am to give to him who sent me." And David said to Gad, "This is a hard decision for me to make. Let us come into the hands of the Lord, for great are his mercies. Let me not come into the hands of men." So David made selection of the disease. And the time was the days of the grain-cutting, when the disease came among the people, causing the death of seventy thousand men from Dan as far as Beer-sheba.

2 Samuel 24:10-15 ⚅ "Good God, Gad! 70,000 dead in three days! At least we didn't go hungry."

UNSAFE PASSAGE
Unsuitable for Student-Led Prayer

And of Jezebel the Lord said, "**Jezebel will become food for dogs** in the heritage of Jezreel. Any man of the family of Ahab who comes to his death in the town will become food for the dogs, and he who comes to his death in the open country will be food for the birds of the air."

1 Kings 21:23-24 ⚅ How many holy scriptures can boast of having the dreaded dog-food-curse?

Woe be to the nation that riseth up against my people, for the Lord almighty will take revenge on them. In the day of judgment he will visit them, for he will give fire and **worms into their flesh, that they may burn** and may feel forever.

Judith 16:20-21 ⚅ The eternal burning you'd get used to, but worms inside you—no thanks.

Yet his food in his bowels is turned. It is cobra venom within him. **He has swallowed down riches**, and he shall vomit them up again. God will cast them out of his belly. He shall suck cobra venom. The viper's tongue shall kill him.

Job 20:14-16 ⚅ Woe to the wicked of yore. Today's wicked don't know how good they've got it.

God is a righteous judge, yes, **a God who has indignation every day**. If a man doesn't relent, he will sharpen his sword. He has bent and strung his bow. He has also prepared for himself the instruments of death. He makes ready his flaming arrows.

Psalms 7:11-13 🕮 *A sad fact of life, even for all-powerful deities, is that all the sword-wielding skills in the world are wasted if you don't take the time to sharpen your blade in advance.*

Let thy hand be found by all thy enemies. Let thy right hand find out all them that hate thee. Thou shalt make them as **an oven of fire** in the time of thy anger. The Lord shall trouble them in his wrath, and fire shall devour them.

Psalms 21:8-9 🕮 *Would God still hate my enemies if I were the world's biggest jerk and my enemies all had really good reasons to hate me?*

God shall break in pieces their teeth in their mouth. The Lord shall break the grinders of the lions. They shall come to nothing, like water running down. He hath bent his bow till they be weakened. Let them be like a snail which melteth and passeth away, like the stillborn child, who has not seen the sun.

Psalms 58:6-8 🕮 *God is love . . . just don't get on his bad side (or you may melt like a snail).*

Thou art terrible, and who shall resist thee when thou art angry?
Psalms 76:7 🕮 *Only in the Bible can you get away with calling God terrible.*

Psalms 76:7

God Is Terrible! *in a good way*

UNLIKELY SIGN
From a Fan in the Stands

And I will feed thy enemies **with their own flesh**, and they shall be drunken with their own blood, as with sweet wine. And all flesh shall know that I, Jehovah, am thy Savior and thy Redeemer, the Mighty One of Jacob.

Isaiah 49:26 🕮 *This may be Monday morning quarterbacking, but might it not be simpler for God to just prevent the oppression in the first place?*

And I will accomplish my fury, and will cause my indignation to rest upon them, and **I will be comforted**. And they shall know that I the Lord have spoken it in my zeal, when I shall have accomplished my indignation in them.

Ezekiel 5:13 🕮 *Who doesn't feel better after accomplishing their fury?*

And the word of Jehovah came unto me, saying, "Son of man, prophesy and say that thus saith Jehovah, 'A sword, a sword, **it is sharpened, and also polished**. It is sharpened that it may make a slaughter. It is polished that it may be as lightning. Shall we then make mirth? The rod of my son, it despises every tree. And it is given to be polished, that it may be handled. The sword, it is sharpened, yea, it is polished, to give it into the hand of the slayer.'"

NEVER ON A SUNDAY SCHOOL'S READING LIST

Ezekiel 21:8-11 🕮 *So to review, it's 1. Sharpen, 2. Polish, 3. Slaughter.*

ANGRY JESUS

Jesus didn't gain followers just by handing out free lunches to the multitudes and telling cryptic stories. He really grabbed people's attention by displaying his righteous anger that he felt toward temple merchants, assorted hypocrites, and fig trees that displeased him. Maybe less well known is his love of swords and his hatred for such things as one's own life.

"Don't think that I came to send peace on the earth. **I didn't come to send peace**, but a sword. For I came to set a man at odds against his father, and the daughter against her mother, and the daughter-in-law against her mother-in-law. A man's foes will be those of his own household."

Matthew 10:34-36 📖 *Is this why so many women have trouble with their mothers-in-law?*

NEVER ON A SUNDAY SCHOOL'S READING LIST

The Bible in Headlines

Trees advised: beware of hungry Jesus
His followers, accustomed to healing miracles, surprised by fig tree's instantaneous death

JERUSALEM, Judea - Now in the morning as he returned to the city, he hungered. And seeing a fig tree by the wayside, he came to it and found nothing thereon but leaves only, and he saith unto it, "**Let there be no fruit from thee** henceforward forever." And immediately the fig tree withered away. And when the disciples saw it, they marvelled, saying, "How did the fig tree immediately wither away?" And Jesus answered and said unto them, "Verily I say unto you, if ye have faith, and doubt not, ye shall not only do what is done to the fig tree, but even if ye shall say unto this mountain, 'Be thou taken up and cast into the sea,' it shall be done."

Matthew 21:18-21 📖 *Jesus wanted his disciples to move mountains, but they couldn't even accomplish something easy like agreeing on when the fig tree died. In Mark 11:12-21 it dies overnight.*

"For then shall there be great tribulation, such as has not been from the beginning of the world until now, nor ever shall be. Truly I say to you, **this generation shall not pass** till all these things be fulfilled."

Matthew 24:21,34 📖 *After Jesus made his apocalyptic prediction, he warned us that no one but the Father knows its exact day or hour (or, evidently, which generation it will happen to).*

And Jesus said, "**For judgment** I am come into this world, that they which see not might see, and that they which see might be made blind."
Luke 9:39 📖 *A guy famous for making the blind see wanted to be known for making the seeing blind.*

And turning round, he said to them, "If any man comes to me and has not **hate for his father and mother** and wife and children and brothers and sisters, and even for his life, he may not be my disciple."
Luke 14:26 📖 *So remember, it's love your enemies and hate your loved ones.*

TOP TEN
The Best of the Worst

But bring those enemies of mine who didn't want me to reign over them here and **kill them before me**.
Luke 19:27 📖 *Jesus wraps up a heartwarming parable with this not-so-veiled threat.*

And he said to them, "But now, he who has a money-bag, or a bag for food, let him take it. And he who has not, let him give his coat for money and **get a sword**."

And they said, "Lord, **here are two swords**." And he said, "It is enough."
Luke 22:36,38 📖 *It doesn't say anywhere that they weren't simply using the swords to practice their fencing skills.*

BIBLE FUNMENTIONABLE QUIZ

W.D.J.S. WHAT DID JESUS SAY?

Everyone knows the sayings of Jesus, right? See if you can fill in the correct word from these less popular quotes of Jesus.

1 "Here are two _____." And he said, "It is enough."
2 "Leave the _____ to bury their own dead."
3 "Don't think that I came to send _____ on the earth."
4 "I didn't come to send peace, but a _____."
5 "For I came to set a man at odds against his _____."
6 "If any man comes to me and has not _____ for his father."
7 And he saith unto the fig tree, "Let there be no _____ from thee."
8 "Let him give his coat for money and get a _____."

hate
sword
dead
swords
sword
father
peace
fruit

1 swords; 2 dead; 3 peace; 4 sword; 5 father; 6 hate; 7 fruit; 8 sword

KILLING

"Thou shalt not kill" sounds nice in theory, but the Bible seems to prefer capital punishment as a way to deal with its most serious offenses. Well, not all of the capital offenses are that serious.

Lamech said to his wives, "Adah and Zillah, hear my voice. You wives of Lamech, listen to my speech, for **I have slain a man for wounding me**, a young man for bruising me."

Genesis 4:23 🎤 *My wives would never let me hear the end of it if I told them that.*

UNSAFE PASSAGE
Unsuitable for Student-Led Prayer

Now the third day was Pharaoh's birthday, and he gave a feast for all his servants, and he gave honor to the chief wine-servant and the chief bread-maker among the others. And he put the chief wine-servant back in his old place, and he gave the cup into Pharaoh's hand. But the **chief bread-maker was put to death** by hanging, as Joseph had said.

Genesis 40:20-22 🎤 *Pharaoh's bakery staff was plagued by a high turnover rate, maybe because his staff appreciation parties sent mixed signals to the survivors.*

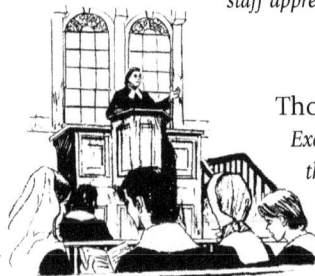

Thou shalt not suffer **a witch** to live.

Exodus 22:18 🎤 *This commandment sure made the world a safer place . . . except for a few thousand innocent women.*

Complete destruction will come on any man who makes offerings to **any other god** but the Lord.

Exodus 22:20 🎤 *At least this once, pagan women must appreciate the Bible's sexist language.*

A man also or a woman that has a familiar spirit, or that is **a wizard**, shall surely be put to death. They shall stone them with stones. Their blood shall be upon them.

Leviticus 20:27 🎤 *When the Bible was written, the people who conjured up spirits weren't just considered to be the charlatans and frauds we know them to be today. One of them actually brings Samuel back from the dead for a vision in 1 Samuel 28:7-15.*

When the tabernacle is to move, the Levites shall take it down, and when the tabernacle is to be set up, the Levites shall set it up. **The stranger who comes near** shall be put to death.

Numbers 1:51 🕮 If the stranger comes near when the tabernacle is being set up, the Levites shall kill him, but if the stranger comes near when the tabernacle is being taken down, the Levites shall kill him.

For everyone who **curses his father or his mother** shall surely be put to death. He has cursed his father or his mother. His blood shall be on him.

The man who **commits adultery** with another man's wife, even he who commits adultery with his neighbor's wife, the adulterer and the adulteress shall surely be put to death.

The man who **lies with his father's wife** has uncovered his father's nakedness. Both of them shall surely be put to death. Their blood shall be on them.

If a man **lie with his daughter-in-law**, both of them shall surely be put to death. They have created confusion. Their blood shall be on them.

If a man **lie with mankind**, as with womankind, both of them have committed abomination. They shall surely be put to death. Their blood shall be on them.

If a man **take a wife and her mother**, it is wickedness. They shall be burnt with fire, both he and they, that there be no wickedness among you.

If a man **lie with an animal**, he shall surely be put to death, and you shall kill the animal.

If a woman **approach to any animal**, and lie down thereto, you shall kill the woman and the animal. They shall surely be put to death. Their blood shall be on them.

Leviticus 20:9-16 🕮 Presumably, ancient animals were much more capable of expressing their consent than your modern animal is.

God commands death to anyone who mentions converting to other religions

Take matters into your own hands, don't call the authorities first

JERUSALEM, Judea - If thy brother, the son of thy mother, or thy son, or thy daughter, or the wife of thy bosom, or thy friend, that is as thine own soul, entice thee secretly, saying, "**Let us go and serve other gods**," which thou hast not known, thou, nor thy fathers, of the gods of the peoples that are round about you, nigh unto thee, or far off from thee, from the one end of the earth even unto the other end of the earth, thou shalt not consent unto him, nor hearken unto him. Neither shall thine eye pity him, neither shalt thou spare, neither shalt thou conceal him, but thou shalt surely kill him. Thy hand shall be first upon him to put him to death, and afterwards the hand of all the people.

Deuteronomy 13:6-9 🕮 *If only all religions had this rule, there would be a lot fewer people pushing their religion door-to-door.*

But he that will be proud and refuse to obey **the commandment of the priest**, who ministereth at that time to the Lord thy God, and the decree of the judge, that man shall die, and thou shalt take away the evil from Israel.

Deuteronomy 17:12 🕮 *Good evidence that Deuteronomy was written by someone from the priesthood.*

*I*f a man is taken in the act of going in to a married woman, the two of them, the man as well as the woman, are to be put to death. So you are to put away the evil from Israel.

Deuteronomy 22:22

Bible Funmentionables Poster Series

EARLY MANDATORY SENTENCING GUIDELINES

The Bible is extremely clear about when you've committed the ultimate crimes. No slap on the wrist. No time off for good behavior.

Thou **shalt kill** for the following offenses:

Not impregnating a widowed sister-in-law
Genesis 38:8-10

Touching the mountain that God is appearing on
Exodus 19:11-13

Smiting your parents
Exodus 21:15

Kidnapping and selling a man
Exodus 21:16

Cursing your parents
Exodus 21:17

Owning an ox that fatally gores someone when the owner knew it was likely to attack
Exodus 21:29

Witchcraft
Exodus 22:18

Worshipping other gods
Exodus 22:20

Working on the sabbath
Exodus 31:14-15

Sleeping with your mother or stepmother
Leviticus 20:11

Sleeping with your daughter-in-law
Leviticus 20:12

Homosexuality (men only)
Leviticus 20:13

Sleeping with your wife and mother-in-law
Leviticus 20:14

Bestiality
Leviticus 20:15-16

Becoming a prostitute (only if you're a priest's daughter)
Leviticus 21:9

Blaspheming the name of the Lord
Leviticus 24:16

Gathering sticks on the sabbath
Numbers 15:32-36

In battle, kill everyone (except the virgins)
Numbers 31:17-18

Attempted religious conversion
Deuteronomy 13:6-9

Disobeying a priest
Deuteronomy 17:12

Falsely prophesying
Deuteronomy 18:20

Rebelling against your parents
Deuteronomy 21:18-21

Turning out not to be a virgin (females only)
Deuteronomy 22:20-21

Having an affair with a married woman
Deuteronomy 22:22

Urban rape victims who don't shout for help loudly enough
Deuteronomy 22:23

Rural rapists
Deuteronomy 22:25-27

Kidnapping and selling a fellow Israelite
Deuteronomy 24:7

VIOLENCE

A regular infusion of gore and destruction is a surefire way to enliven your otherwise boring old scriptures or youth hockey league championship. But when it's your supreme being that approves of such acts, it can have the unintended (or intended) consequence of convincing the faithful that committing a horrible injustice is justified and sometimes even the key to salvation.

UNSAFE PASSAGE
Unsuitable for Student-Led Prayer

And when Phinees the son of Eleazar, the son of Aaron the priest, saw it, he rose up from the midst of the multitude. And **taking a dagger**, he went in after the Israelite into the brothel house and thrust both of them through together, to wit, the man and the woman in the genital parts. And the scourge ceased from the children of Israel.

Numbers 25:7-8 ⚰ *Reason enough to stay out of those brothel houses.*

And when the Lord has given them up into your hands, and you have overcome them, give them up to **complete destruction**. Make no agreement with them, and have no mercy on them. Do not take wives or husbands from among them. Do not give your daughters to their sons, or take their daughters for your sons. For through them your sons will be turned from me to the worship of other gods, and the Lord will be moved to wrath against you and send destruction on you quickly. But this is what you are to do to them: their altars are to be pulled down, and their pillars broken, and their Asherah poles cut down, and their images burned with fire.

Deuteronomy 7:2-5 ⚰ *Loose translation: Kill them before they convert you to another religion.*

But the Lord sent destruction on seventy men of the people of Beth-shemesh **for looking into the ark** of the Lord. And great was the sorrow of the people for the destruction which the Lord had sent on them.

1 Samuel 6:19 ⚰ *"If I catch any of you guys in my stuff, I'll kill you." –Francis Sawyer*

Now on the day after, when the Philistines came to take their goods from the dead, they saw Saul and his three sons dead on the earth in Mount Gilboa. And **cutting off his head** and taking away his war-dress, they sent word into the land of the Philistines round about, to take the news to their gods and to the people.

1 Samuel 31:8-9 ⚰ *Before mass media you had to publicize your killings the old fashioned way.*

And Nahash the Ammonite answered them, "On this condition will I make a covenant with you, that I may **thrust out all your right eyes**, and lay it for a reproach upon all Israel."

1 Samuel 11:2 ▩ *"But then our 3-D glasses won't work!"*

And again Abner said to Asahel, "Go off, and do not follow me, lest I be obliged to stab thee to the ground, and I shall not be able to hold up my face to Joab thy brother." But he refused to hearken to him and would not turn aside; wherefore Abner struck him with his spear with a **back stroke in the groin**, and thrust him through, and he died upon the spot. And all those who came to the place where Asahel fell down and died, they stood still.

2 Samuel 2:22-23 ▩ *Every stalker preparedness class should teach the old backstroke groin thrusts.*

And when Abner was returned to Hebron, Joab took him aside to the middle of the gate, to speak to him treacherously, and **he stabbed him there in the groin**, and he died in revenge of the blood of Asahel his brother.

2 Samuel 3:27 ▩ *I hate getting stabbed there . . . right in the middle of the gate.*

And they entered into the house secretly taking ears of corn. And Rechab and Baana his brother **stabbed him in the groin** and fled away.

2 Samuel 4:6 ▩ *But really, how hard is it to outrun a guy that you just stabbed in the groin?*

Thou hast girded me with strength unto the battle. Thou hast subdued under me those that rose up against me. Thou hast also made mine enemies turn their backs unto me, that I might cut off them that hate me. They looked, but there was none to save, even unto Jehovah, but he answered them not. Then did I beat them small as the dust of the earth. I did crush them as the mire of the streets and did spread them abroad.

2 Samuel 22:40-43 ▩ *A warrior yearning to relive those glorious battles of old, but lacking a receptive audience for his blood-thirsty and self-serving exaggerations, has a new and biblically-sanctioned outlet: the prayer of thanksgiving to the Lord.*

And Elijah in answer said to the captain of fifty, "**If I am a man of God**, may fire come down from heaven on you and on your fifty men and put an end to you." Then fire came down from heaven and put an end to him and his fifty men. Then the king sent another captain of fifty with his fifty men, and he said to Elijah, "O man of God, the king says, 'Come down quickly.'" And Elijah, in answer, said, "If I am a man of God, may fire come down from heaven on you and on your fifty men and put an end to you." And the fire of God came down from heaven and put an end to him and his fifty men.

2 Kings 1:10-12 ▩ *And then the king sent out <u>another</u> captain of fifty . . .*

WHOLLY UNHOLY
The Dark Side of the Bible

And he said, "Take her and **put her out of the window.**" So they sent her down with force, and her blood went in a shower on the wall and on the horses, and she was crushed under their feet. And he came in and took food and drink. Then he said, "Now see to this cursed woman, and put her body into the earth, for she is a king's daughter." And they went out to put her body into the earth, but nothing of her was to be seen, only the bones of her head, and her feet, and parts of her hands. So they came back and gave him word of it. And he said, "This is what the Lord said by his servant Elijah the Tishbite, saying, 'In the heritage of Jezreel the flesh of Jezebel will become food for dogs, and the dead body of Jezebel will be like waste dropped on the face of the earth in the heritage of Jezreel, so that they will not be able to recognize her as Jezebel.'"

2 Kings 9:33-37 Show respect for the king's daughter: bury her after you throw her out the window.

UNSAFE PASSAGE
Unsuitable for Student-Led Prayer

And when the letter came to them, they took the king's sons and put them to death, all the seventy, and **put their heads in baskets** and sent them to him at Jezreel.

2 Kings 10:7 "I'm pretty sure I said I wanted the <u>breads</u> in baskets."

David took the people of the town and **cut them with saws**, iron picks, and axes. He did so to all the Ammonite cities. Then David and all the troops returned to Jerusalem.

1 Chronicles 20:3 Some translations say that he "put them to work" with saws and axes. It says something about your holy book when both options seem equally plausible.

Now when Jehoram had taken his place over his father's kingdom and had made his position safe, **he put all his brothers to death** with the sword, as well as some of the princes of Israel.

2 Chronicles 21:4 Whoever said the Bible doesn't contain real-world, practical advice for today's modern despot?

For Athalia, his mother, seeing that her son was dead, rose up and **killed all the royal family** of the house of Joram.

2 Chronicles 22:10 Mothers, in today's society, it is actually recommended that you start by calling 911 when you find a dead body.

And all the people **enter the house of Baal** and break it down. Yea, his altars and his images they have broken, and Mattan, the priest of Baal, they have slain before the altars.

2 Chronicles 23:17 Weren't most of Baal's faithful just following the religion that their parents taught them to believe? Nowadays you should at least give them a chance to renounce their religion before you kill them.

And Amasias, taking courage, led forth his people and went to the vale of saltpits, and they slew ten thousand of the children of Seir. And another ten thousand men the sons of Judah took and brought to the steep of a certain rock, and he **cast them down headlong** from the top, and they all were broken to pieces.

2 Chronicles 25:11-12 ☠ Amasias' people and Judah's sons make killing 20,000 people seem way easier than it actually is!

But **God shall break the heads of his enemies**, the hairy crown of them that walk on in their sins. The Lord said, "I will turn them from Basan. I will turn them into the depth of the sea, that thy foot may be dipped in the blood of thy enemies, and the tongue of thy dogs be red with the same."

Psalms 68:21-23 ☠ "I'm not wading in a pool of blood that my dog had his tongue in."

Blessed be he that shall take and dash thy little ones against the rock.

Psalms 137:9 ☠ Write this sentiment in the Bible, and people will revere it. Write it in a school essay, and you'll be suspended and evaluated.

Therefore, **deliver up their children to the famine**, and give them over to the power of the sword, and let their wives become childless and widows. And let their men be slain of death and their young men smitten of the sword in battle. Let a cry be heard from their houses, when thou shalt bring a troop suddenly upon them. For they have dug a pit to take me and hid snares for my feet. Yet, Jehovah, thou knowest all their counsel against me to slay me. Forgive not their iniquity, neither blot out their sin from thy sight. But let them be overthrown before thee. Deal thou with them in the time of thine anger.

Jeremiah 18:21-23 ☠ Praying for good things to happen for yourself looks positively saintly when compared to praying that your enemies' sins not be forgiven.

Then was the king exceeding glad for him, and he commanded that Daniel should be taken out of the den. And Daniel was taken out of the den, and no hurt was found in him, because he believed in his God. And by the king's commandment, those men were brought that bad accused Daniel, and they were cast into the lions' den, **they and their children and their wives**. And they did not reach the bottom of the den, before the lions caught them and broke all their bones in pieces.

Daniel 6:23-24 ☠ Do children's Bibles include the thrilling conclusion of Daniel in the lion's den?

And I will **kill her children with death**, and all the churches shall know that I am he which searcheth the reins and hearts. And I will give unto every one of you according to your works.

Revelation 2:23 ☠ If there's a better way to kill children, I haven't heard it.

WAR

The Bible teems with examples that demonstrate one thing: Jehovah loved war. Early authors of the Bible were eager to convince the people that their victory or defeat in war depended entirely upon whether they followed all of the rules that these same authors had written down. And if that didn't convince you to fight the non-believers, you were commanded to take their land and their virgins. So the recruitment poster could have read, "Come for the piety. Stay for the virgins."

Say to the children of Israel, "When you go over Jordan into the land of Canaan, see that all the people of the land are **forced out from before you**. And put to destruction all their pictured stones, and all their metal images, and all their high places. And take the land for yourselves and dwell in it. For to you I have given the land as your heritage, and you will take up your heritage in the land by the decision of the Lord, to every family its part. The greater the family the greater its heritage, and the smaller the family the smaller will be its heritage. Wherever the decision of the Lord gives to any man his part, that will be his. Distribution will be made to you by your fathers' tribes. But if you are slow in driving out the people of the land, then those of them who are still there will be like pin-points in your eyes and like thorns in your sides, troubling you in the land where you are living. And it will come about that as it was my purpose to do to them, so I will do to you."

Numbers 33:51-56 📖 The Bible gives you the who, when, where, why, and how of ethnic cleansing and even throws in a what-happens-if-you-don't!

WHOLLY UNHOLY
The Dark Side of the Bible

And the Lord said to me, "See, from now on I have given Sihon and his land into your hands. Go forward now to take his land and make it yours." Then Sihon came out against us with all his people, to make an attack on us at Jahaz. And the Lord our God gave him into our hands, and we overcame him and his sons and all his people. At that time we took all his towns and gave them over to **complete destruction**, together with men, women, and children. We had no mercy on any.

Deuteronomy 2:31-34 📖 Back then it was a divine decree. Today we tend to call it a war crime.

And Abijah and his people slew them with a great slaughter, so there fell down slain of Israel **500,000 valiant men**.

2 Chronicles 13:17 📖 This passage helped to push the "Killings in the Bible committed or condoned by God" total into the 2.4 million range! With 31,102 verses, that brings the average to just over 77 human beings killed per Bible verse (excluding the unnumbered dead in mass extinctions like the great flood).

When Jehoshaphat and his people came to take the spoil of them, they found among them in abundance **both riches and dead bodies**, and precious jewels, which they stripped off for themselves, more than they could carry away. And they were three days in taking the spoil, it was so much.

2 Chronicles 20:25 ⚔ *By the third day of plundering corpse jewels, I bet you really had to work your booty off.*

And the other Jews that were in the king's provinces gathered themselves together, and stood for their lives, and had rest from their enemies, and **slew of them that hated them** seventy and five thousand, but on the spoil they laid not their hand.

Esther 9:16 ⚔ *A courteous soldier never takes the spoils of war (after killing 75,000 people).*

Now the thirteenth day of the month Adar was the first day with them all of the slaughter, and on the fourteenth day they rested, which they ordained to be kept as a holy day, so that all times hereafter they should celebrate it with feasting and gladness. But they that were killing in the city of Shushan were **employed in the slaughter** on the thirteenth and fourteenth day of the same month, and on the fifteenth day they rested. And therefore they appointed that day to be a holy day of feasting and gladness.

Esther 9:17-18 ⚔ *A happy post-slaughter holiday to all!*

Arise, why sleepest thou, O Lord? Arise, and cast us not off to the end. **Why turnest thou face away** and forgettest our want and our trouble? Our soul is humbled down to the dust. Our belly cleaveth to the earth.

Psalms 44:23-25 ⚔ *Translation: Whenever we win in battle, that proves our God is invincible. When we lose, he was just taking a nap.*

PSALMS 44:23
God Is Asleep!
UNLIKELY SIGN
From a Fan in the Stands

BIBLE FUNMENTIONABLES QUIZ

SLAUGHTER IS THE BLEST MEDICINE

The Bible doesn't shy away from the S-word, in fact it openly promotes slaughter. But do you know when the time is right for a good slaughtering? Fill in the blanks below with either **SLAUGHTER** or **LAUGHTER**.

1 I said of _____, it is mad. *Ecclesiastes 2:2*

2 For now hath there been no great _____ among the Philistines. *1 Samuel 14:30*

3 Even in _____ the heart is sorrowful. *Proverbs 14:13*

4 Ye have nourished your hearts in a day of _____. *James 5:5*

5 He will yet fill thy mouth with _____ and thy lips with shouting. *Job 8:21*

6 Sorrow is better than _____. *Ecclesiastes 7:3*

7 For as the crackling of thorns under a pot, so is the _____ of the fool. *Ecclesiastes 7:6*

8 And the revolters are gone deep in making _____. *Hosea 5:2*

1 Laughter, 2 Slaughter, 3 Laughter, 4 Slaughter, 5 Laughter, 6 Laughter, 7 Laughter, 8 Slaughter

EVIL

Believers in an all-knowing, all-powerful being sometimes wonder why God allows so much evil. He knows it's going to happen, he could stop it if he wanted, but yet we still have deadly tsunamis, earthquakes, famines, and boneheaded backyard stunts gone terribly wrong. It was an issue for the writers of the Bible, just as it is for us today.

And whenever **the evil spirit from God** came on Saul, David took his instrument and made music. So new life came to Saul, and he got well, and the evil spirit went away from him.

> 1 Samuel 16:23 🔖 *Like a vampire's aversion to sunlight, God's evil spirit can't stand music. Or maybe David's music was actually really, really bad.*

Wherefore I will pray to the Lord and address my speech to God, who doth great things and unsearchable and wonderful things without number. He giveth rain upon the face of the earth and watereth all things with waters. He setteth up the humble on high and comforteth with health those that mourn. **He bringeth to nought the designs of the malignant**, so that their hands cannot accomplish what they had begun.

> Job 5:8-12 🔖 *If God stops all evil acts, then a successful evil plot would seem to have either slipped past him somehow, or it would have some kind of divine tacit approval.*

▶ ▶ **UNSAFE PASSAGE**
Unsuitable for Student-Led Prayer

Why is life given to the evil-doers? Why do they become old and strong in power? Their children are ever with them, and their offspring are before their eyes. Their houses are free from fear, and the rod of God does not come on them. Their ox is ready at all times to give seed. Their cow gives birth without dropping her young. They send out their young ones like a flock, and their children have pleasure in the dance. They make songs to the instruments of music and are glad at the sound of the pipe. Their days come to an end without trouble, and suddenly they go down to the underworld, though they said to God, "Go away from us, for we have no desire for the knowledge of your ways. What is the Ruler of all, that we may give him worship? And what profit is it to us to make prayer to him?"

> Job 21:7-15 🔖 *It definitely seems like a reasonable request of God that he makes the evil-doers' children not be glad at the sound of the pipe and that their cows every so often drop their young.*

UNLIKELY SIGN
From a Fan in the Stands

Ecclesiastes 8:14
Evil Happens

There is also another vanity which is done upon the earth. There are just men to whom **evils happen**, as though they had done the works of the wicked. And there are wicked men, who are as secure as though they had done the deeds of the just. But this also I judge most vain.

Ecclesiastes 8:14 ⚰ *All the vanities listed in Ecclesiastes prove that you really can find lots of meaninglessness in the Bible.*

I form the light and create darkness. I make peace and **create evil**. I am Yahweh who does all these things.

Isaiah 45:7 ⚰ *"Why is there evil in the world, Mommy?"*

TOP TEN
The Best of the Worst

Now some people who were there at that time, gave him an account of how the blood of some Galilaeans had been mixed by Pilate with their offerings. And he, in answer, said to them, "Are you of the opinion that these Galilaeans were worse than all other Galilaeans, because these things were done to them? I say to you, it is not so. But if your hearts are not changed, you will all come to the same end. Or those **eighteen men who were crushed** by the fall of the tower of Siloam, were they worse than all the other men living in Jerusalem? I say to you, it is not so. But if your hearts are not changed, you will all come to an end in the same way."

Luke 13:1-5 ⚰ *Jesus says that bad things happen to some people for no good reason. Oh, and if you don't have a change of heart, you'll get crushed by a tower.*

We know that we are of God, and the whole world lies in **the power of the Evil One**.

1 John 5:19 ⚰ *"The whole world" in all likelihood means "the whole world except for us."*

*W*ounding blows cleanse away evil, and beatings purge the innermost parts.

Proverbs 20:30

Bible Funmentionables Poster Series

FAMILY

Many people try to use the Bible to prove that their point of view on a contemporary issue is correct. Nowhere is this more prevalent than among those who like to promote the Bible's family values. The quotes below show that there is actually a wide variety of family values, including the unsettling impression that Jesus showed less devotion to his own mother than most of his followers do.

And Jephthah took an oath to the Lord, and said, "If you will give the children of Ammon into my hands, then whoever comes out from the door of my house, meeting me when I come back in peace from the children of Ammon, will be the Lord's, and I will give him *__as a burned offering__.*" Then Jephthah came back to his house in Mizpah, and his daughter came out, meeting him on his way with music and with dances. She was his only child. He had no other sons or daughters. And when he saw her he was overcome with grief and said, "Ah! my daughter! I am crushed with sorrow, and it is you who are the chief cause of my trouble, for I have made an oath to the Lord, and I may not take it back." And she said to him, "My father, you have made an oath to the Lord. Do then to me whatever you have said, for the Lord has sent a full reward on your haters, on the children of Ammon." And he said, "Go then." So he sent her away for two months. So she departed with her companions and mourned her virginity on the mountains. And at the end of two months she went back to her father, who did with her as he had said in his oath, and she had never been touched by a man. So it became a rule in Israel, for the women to go year by year sorrowing for the daughter of Jephthah the Gileadite, four days in every year.

Judges 11:30-31,34-36,38-40 📖 *It seems that the moral here is don't promise God anything stupid, because he'll expect you to come through, even if it entails incinerating your own child.*

BIBLE FUNMENTIONABLES QUIZ

WHO BEGAT?

Can you recognize the actual descendants of Noah from the impostors in the list below?

Shem	Reu	Tubal	Kittim	Nimrod	Lehabim	Peleg	Diklah	Banania
Ham	Japheth	Meshech	Dodanim	Vive	Naphtuhim	Joktan	Ophir	Joktan
Phut	Gomer	Ashkenaz	Raamah	Babel	Pathrusim	Smorz	Hazarmaveth	Serug
Cush	Weetos	Riphath	Chocos	Erech	Casluhim	Almodad	Jobab	Nahor
Kix	Magog	Togarmah	Sabtecha	Ludim	Caphtorim	Sheleph		
Heth	Javan	Tarshish	Dedan	Anamim	Arphaxad	Uzal		

Kix, Weetos, Chocos, Vive, Smorz, & Banania are breakfast cereals.

TOP TEN
The Best of the Worst

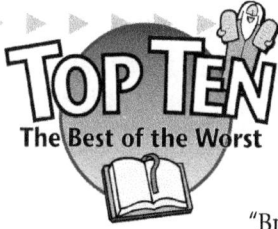

As they were making their hearts merry, behold, the men of the city, certain base fellows, beset the house round about, beating at the door. And they spoke to the master of the house, the old man, saying, "Bring forth the man who came into your house, that we may know him."

The man, the master of the house, went out to them, and said to them, "No, my brothers, please don't act so wickedly. Seeing that this man is come into my house, don't do this folly. Behold, here is my daughter, a virgin, and his concubine. Them I will bring out now, and humble you them, and **do with them what seems good to you**, but to this man don't do any such folly." But the men wouldn't listen to him, so the man took hold of his concubine, and brought her forth to them, and they knew her, and abused her all the night until the morning. And when the day began to spring, they let her go. When he was come into his house, he took a knife, and laid hold on his concubine, and divided her limb by limb into twelve pieces, and sent her throughout all the borders of Israel.

Judges 19:22-25,29 📖 Just when you think the story couldn't get any worse, she gets cut up into twelve pieces — twelve being a spiritually significant number representing governmental perfection.

And when David heard that Nabal was dead, he said, "**Blessed be the Lord**, that hath pleaded the cause of my reproach from the hand of Nabal, and hath kept his servant from evil. For the Lord hath returned the wickedness of Nabal upon his own head." And David sent and communed with Abigail, to take her to him to wife.

1 Samuel 25:39 📖 David is so excited when Abigail's husband dies, it's as if he heard that they just got a new shipment in at Wives-R-Us. Some people collect women's shoes, others collect women.

And the king said to her, "What is troubling you?" And she said in answer, "This woman said to me, 'Give your son to be our food today, and we will have my son to-morrow.' So **we boiled my son** and did eat him. And I said unto her on the next day, 'Give thy son, that we may eat him.' And she hath hid her son."

2 Kings 6:29 📖 "She said she really didn't feel like eating boy two nights in a row."

My breath is offensive

to my wife. I am loathsome to the children of my own mother.

Job 19:17 📖 We all knew Job had it rough, but bad breath on top of everything else? So cruel.

And I will cause them to eat the flesh of their sons and the flesh of their daughters, and they shall eat everyone the flesh of his friend.

Jeremiah 19:9

*A*nd the Lord said unto Moses, "If her father had but spit in her face, should she not be ashamed seven days? Let her be shut out from the camp seven days, and after that let her be received in again."

Numbers 12:14   Bible Funmentionables Poster Series

Give thy son his way, and he shall make thee afraid. Play with him, and he shall make thee sorrowful. **Laugh not with him**, lest thou have sorrow, and at the last thy teeth be set on edge. Give him not liberty in his youth, and wink not at his devices. Bow down his neck while he is young, and beat his sides while he is a child, lest he grow stubborn, and regard thee not, and so be a sorrow of heart to thee.

> Sirach 30:9-12 ☠ *Ah, the age-old parenting class motto: "Less laughing, more beating!"*

While he was yet speaking to the multitudes, behold, his mother and his brethren stood without, seeking to speak to him. And one said unto him, "Behold, thy mother and thy brethren stand without, seeking to speak to thee." But he answered and said unto him that told him, "**Who is my mother?** and who are my brethren?" And he stretched forth his hand towards his disciples and said, "Behold, my mother and my brethren! For whosoever shall do the will of my Father who is in heaven, he is my brother, and sister, and mother."

> Matthew 12:46-50 ☠ *So avoiding some of your mom's constant phone calls does have some biblical precedent.*

GOD'S ODDS CATS vs. UNICORNS
Which are you more likely to find in the Bible?

☠ Picking up a Bible and reading a passage at random may not lead to immediate enlightenment (go see for yourself), but what topics are you more or less likely to stumble upon? Here are the odds of randomly finding a verse on some favorite biblical themes.

More likely		vs.	Less likely		More likely		vs.	Less likely	
MAN	1 in 7	vs.	WOMAN	1 in 90	STRONG	1 in 120	vs.	WEAK	1 in 546
WAR	1 in 25	vs.	PEACE	1 in 74	KILL/SMITE	1 in 90	vs.	FORGIVE	1 in 327
GOD	1 in 7	vs.	GODS	1 in 275	OBEY	1 in 130	vs.	REBEL	1 in 273
LOVE	1 in 70	vs.	HATE	1 in 74	DRUNK	1 in 403	vs.	SOBER	1 in 2,073
DESTROY	1 in 72	vs.	CREATE	1 in 691	UNICORN	1 in 3,456	vs.	CAT	0 in 31,102

And Peter said, "See, we have given up what is ours to come after you." And he said to them, "Truly I say to you, there is no man who has **given up house or wife** or brothers or father or mother or children, because of the kingdom of God, who will not get much more in this time and in the world to come, eternal life." *Luke 18:28-30* 🪦 *Ever feel like ditching the wife and family? Just remember to do it for the kingdom of God, and you're set for life—and beyond!*

THESE ARE THE DESCENDANTS

THE MOST BORING STORY EVER TOLD

Genealogies are a Bible specialty, but they are exceedingly difficult to gain any spiritual insights from. Give it a try with Genesis 10 and 11:10-32. Once you have finished with that, you're ready for the big leagues. Gather the family around and read 1 Chronicles, chapters 1-9. (See the next two pages for just some of the excitement.)

After reading all of that, you can be thankful you were not one of those monks who had to handwrite and decorate these less than spiritually enriching chapters.

969 YEARS YOUNG!

🪦 These days, when an older man fathers a child, it is considered by many to be unfair to the child, since the father won't be around for much of the child's life. Not so in the old days.

Name	Became a father at the age of	Died at the age of
Adam	130	930*
The father of		
Seth	105	912
The father of		
Enosh	90	905
The father of		
Kenan	70	910**
The father of		
Mahalalel	65	895
The father of		
Jared	162	962***
The father of		
Enoch	65	365****
The father of		
Methuselah	187	969
The father of		
Lamech	182	777
The father of		
Noah	500*****	950

* Adam could've met his great-great-great-great-great-great grandson, Lamech. ("Back in _my_ day, we didn't have all these multiple wives you see today. Do you know how hard it was to find women for my sons to marry?") There's no mention of when Eve died.

** We should all be so lucky to live long enough to witness our child turn 840 years old.

*** It's sad to see a father who outlives his son…by 435 years!

**** Tragically cut down in his prime.

***** Noah is famous for the wrong reason.

WORST BABY NAME EVER?

Isaiah must have had second thoughts about God's unsolicited name suggestion in the verse below. Not only is it a bit on the long side (the longest word in the Bible), but it also loosely translates to "Loot quickly and take the prey." How to Mess Up a Kid 101.

🪦 And I went to the prophetess, and she conceived, and bare a son. Then said the Lord to me, "Call his name Mahershalalhashbaz." *Isaiah 8:3*

The To-Be-Read-Aloud Bible Study Challenge: 1 Chronicles 1, 2, 3 …

Adam, Sheth, Enosh, Kenan, Mahalaleel, Jered, Henoch, Methuselah, Lamech, Noah, Shem, Ham, and Japheth. The sons of Japheth; Gomer, and Magog, and Madai, and Javan, and Tubal, and Meshech, and Tiras. And the sons of Gomer; Ashchenaz, and Riphath, and Togarmah. And the sons of Javan; Elishah, and Tarshish, Kittim, and Dodanim. The sons of Ham; Cush, and Mizraim, Put, and Canaan. The sons of Cush; Seba, and Havilah, and Sabta, and Raamah, and Sabtecha. And the sons of Raamah; Sheba, and Dedan. And Cush begat Nimrod: he began to be mighty upon the earth. And Mizraim begat Ludim, and Anamim, and Lehabim, and Naphtuhim, And Pathrusim, and Casluhim, (of whom came the Philistines,) and Caphthorim. And Canaan begat Zidon his firstborn, and Heth, The Jebusite also, and the Amorite, and the Girgashite, And the Hivite, and the Arkite, and the Sinite, And the Arvadite, and the Zemarite, and the Hamathite. The sons of Shem; Elam, and Asshur, and Arphaxad, and Lud, and Aram, and Uz, and Hul, and Gether, and Meshech. And Arphaxad begat Shelah, and Shelah begat Eber. And unto Eber were born two sons: the name of the one was Peleg; because in his days the earth was divided: and his brother's name was Joktan. And Joktan begat Almodad, and Sheleph, and Hazarmaveth, and Jerah, Hadoram also, and Uzal, and Diklah, And Ebal, and Abimael, and Sheba, And Ophir, and Havilah, and Jobab. All these were the sons of Joktan. Shem, Arphaxad, Shelah, Eber, Peleg, Reu, Serug, Nahor, Terah, Abram; the same is Abraham. The sons of Abraham; Isaac, and Ishmael. These are their generations: The firstborn of Ishmael, Nebaioth; then Kedar, and Adbeel, and Mibsam, Mishma, and Dumah, Massa, Hadad, and Tema, Jetur, Naphish, and Kedemah. These are the sons of Ishmael. Now the sons of Keturah, Abraham's concubine: she bare Zimran, and Jokshan, and Medan, and Midian, and Ishbak, and Shuah. And the sons of Jokshan; Sheba, and Dedan. And the sons of Midian; Ephah, and Epher, and Henoch, and Abida, and Eldaah. All these are the sons of Keturah. And Abraham begat Isaac. The sons of Isaac; Esau and Israel. The sons of Esau; Eliphaz, Reuel, and Jeush, and Jaalam, and Korah. The sons of Eliphaz; Teman, and Omar, Zephi, and Gatam, Kenaz, and Timna, and Amalek. The sons of Reuel; Nahath, Zerah, Shammah, and Mizzah. And the sons of Seir; Lotan, and Shobal, and Zibeon, and Anah, and Dishon, and Ezar, and Dishan. And the sons of Lotan; Hori, and Homam: and Timna was Lotan's sister. The sons of Shobal; Alian, and Manahath, and Ebal, Shephi, and Onam. And the sons of Zibeon; Aiah, and Anah. The sons of Anah; Dishon. And the sons of Dishon; Amram, and Eshban, and Ithran, and Cheran. The sons of Ezer; Bilhan, and Zavan, and Jakan. The sons of Dishan; Uz, and Aran. Now these are the kings that reigned in the land of Edom before any king reigned over the children of Israel; Bela the son of Beor: and the name of his city was Dinhabah. And when Bela was dead, Jobab the son of Zerah of Bozrah reigned in his stead. And when Jobab was dead, Husham of the land of the Temanites reigned in his stead. And when Husham was dead, Hadad the son of Bedad, which smote Midian in the field of Moab, reigned in his stead: and the name of his city was Avith. And when Hadad was dead, Samlah of Masrekah reigned in his stead. And when Samlah was dead, Shaul of Rehoboth by the river reigned in his stead. And when Shaul was dead, Baalhanan the son of Achbor reigned in his stead. And when Baalhanan was dead, Hadad reigned in his stead: and the name of his city was Pai; and his wife's name was Mehetabel, the daughter of Matred, the daughter of Mezahab. Hadad died also. And the dukes of Edom were; Duke Timnah, Duke Aliah, Duke Jetheth, Duke Aholibamah, Duke Elah, Duke Pinon, Duke Kenaz, Duke Teman, Duke Mibzar, Duke Magdiel, Duke Iram. These are the dukes of Edom. Ladies and gentlemen, let's welcome right here on our stage, The Dukes of Edom! These are the sons of Israel; Reuben, Simeon, Levi, and Judah, Issachar, and Zebulun, Dan, Joseph, and Benjamin, Naphtali, Gad, and Asher. The sons of Judah; Er, and Onan, and Shelah: which three were born unto him of the daughter of Shua the Canaanitess. And Er, the firstborn of Judah, was evil in the sight of the Lord; and he slew him. And Tamar his daughter in law bore him Pharez and Zerah. All the sons of Judah were five. The sons of Pharez; Hezron, and Hamul. And the sons of Zerah; Zimri, and Ethan, and Heman, and Calcol, and Dara: five of them in all. And the sons of Carmi; Achar, the troubler of Israel, who transgressed in the thing accursed. Don't you wonder what the thing accursed was. Now that really sounds more interesting than all of these names! And the sons of Ethan; Azariah. The sons also of Hezron, that were born unto him; Jerahmeel, and Ram, and Chelubai. And Ram begat Amminadab; and Amminadab begat Nahshon, prince of the children of Judah; And Nahshon begat Salma, and Salma begat Boaz, And Boaz begat Obed, and Obed begat Jesse, And Jesse begat his firstborn Eliab, and Abinadab the second, and Shimma the third, Nethaneel the fourth, Raddai the fifth, Ozem the sixth, David the seventh: Whose sisters were Zeruiah, and Abigail. And the sons of Zeruiah; Abishai, and Joab, and Asahel, three. And Abigail bare Amasa: and the father of Amasa was Jether the Ishmeelite. And Caleb the son of Hezron begat children of Azubah his wife, and of Jerioth: her sons are these; Jesher, and Shobab, and Ardon. And when Azubah was dead, Caleb took unto him Ephrath, which bare him Hur. And Hur begat Uri, and Uri begat Bezaleel. And afterward Hezron went in to the daughter of Machir the father of Gilead, whom he married when he was threescore years old; and she bare him Segub. And Segub begat Jair, who had three and twenty cities in the land of Gilead. And he took Geshur, and Aram, with the towns of Jair, from them, with Kenath, and the towns thereof, even threescore cities. All these belonged to the sons of Machir the father of Gilead. And after that Hezron was dead in Calebephratah, then Abiah Hezron's wife bare him Ashur the father of Tekoa. And the sons of Jerahmeel the firstborn of Hezron were, Ram the firstborn, and Bunah, and Oren, and Ozem, and Ahijah. Jerahmeel had also another wife, whose name was Atarah; she was the mother of Onam. And the sons of Ram the firstborn of Jerahmeel were, Maaz, and Jamin, and Eker. And the sons of Onam were, Shammai, and Jada. And the sons of Shammai; Nadab, and Abishur. And the name of the wife of Abishur was Abihail, and she bare him Ahban, and Molid. And the sons of Nadab; Seled, and Appaim: but Seled died without children. And the sons of Appaim; Ishi. And the sons of Ishi; Sheshan. And the children of Sheshan; Ahlai. And the sons of Jada the brother of Shammai; Jether, and Jonathan: and Jether died without children. And the sons of Jonathan; Peleth, and Zaza. These were the sons of Jerahmeel. Now Sheshan had no sons, but daughters. Which is such a shame because ain't no way we're gonna list a bunch of girls' names in here! And Sheshan had a servant, an Egyptian, whose name was Jarha. And Sheshan gave his daughter to Jarha his servant to wife; and she bare him Attai. And Attai begat Nathan, and Nathan begat Zabad, And Zabad begat Ephlal, and Ephlal begat Obed, And Obed begat Jehu, and Jehu begat Azariah, And Azariah begat Helez, and Helez begat Eleasah, And Eleasah begat Sisamai, and Sisamai begat Shallum, And Shallum begat Jekamiah, and Jekamiah begat Elishama. Now the sons of Caleb the brother of Jerahmeel were, Mesha his firstborn, which was the father of Ziph; and the sons of Mareshah the father of Hebron. And the sons of Hebron; Korah, and Tappuah, and Rekem, and Shema. And Shema begat Raham, the father of Jorkoam: and Rekem begat Shammai. And the son of Shammai was Maon: and Maon was the father of Bethzur. And Ephah, Caleb's concubine, bare Haran, and Moza, and Gazez: and Haran begat Gazez. And the sons of Jahdai; Regem, and Jotham, and Gesham, and Pelet, and Ephah, and Shaaph. Maachah, Caleb's concubine, bare Sheber, and Tirhanah. She bare also Shaaph the father of Madmannah, Sheva the father of Machbenah, and the father of Gibea: and the daughter of Caleb was Achsa. These were the sons of Caleb the son of Hur, the firstborn of Ephratah; Shobal the father of Kirjathjearim, Salma the father of Bethlehem, Hareph the father of Bethgader. And Shobal the father of Kirjathjearim had sons; Haroeh, and half of the Manahethites. And the families of Kirjathjearim; the Ithrites, and the Puhites, and the Shumathites, and the Mishraites; of them came the Zareathites, and the Eshtaulites. The sons of Salma; Bethlehem, and the Netophathites, Ataroth, the house of Joab, and half of the Manahethites, the Zorites. And the families of the scribes which dwelt at Jabez; the Tirathites, the Shimeathites, and Suchathites. These are the Kenites that came of Hemath, the father of the house of Rechab. Now these were the sons of David, which were born unto him in Hebron; the firstborn Amnon, of Ahinoam the Jezreelitess; the second Daniel, of Abigail the Carmelitess: The third, Absalom the son of Maachah the daughter of Talmai king of Geshur: the fourth, Adonijah the son of Haggith: The fifth, Shephatiah of Abital: the sixth, Ithream by Eglah his wife. These six were born unto him in Hebron; and there he reigned seven years and

On that night could not the king sleep, and he commanded to bring the

six months: and in Jerusalem he reigned thirty three years. And these were born unto him in Jerusalem; Shimea, and Shobab, and Nathan, and Solomon, four, of Bathshua the daughter of Ammiel: Ibhar also, and Elishama, and Eliphelet, And Nogah, and Nepheg, and Japhia, And Elishama, and Eliada, and Eliphelet, nine. These were all the sons of David, beside the sons of the concubines, and Tamar their sister. And Solomon's son was Rehoboam, Abia his son, Asa his son, Jehoshaphat his son, Joram his son, Ahaziah his son, Joash his son, Amaziah his son, Azariah his son, Jotham his son, Ahaz his son, Hezekiah his son, Manasseh his son, Amon his son, Josiah his son. And the sons of Josiah were, the firstborn Johanan, the second Jehoiakim, the third Zedekiah, the fourth Shallum. And the sons of Jehoiakim: Jeconiah his son, Zedekiah his son. And the sons of Jeconiah; Assir, Salathiel his son, Malchiram also, and Pedaiah, and Shenazar, Jecamiah, Hoshama, and Nedabiah. And the sons of Pedaiah were, Zerubbabel, and Shimei: and the sons of Zerubbabel; Meshullam, and Hananiah, and Shelomith their sister: And Hashubah, and Ohel, and Berechiah, and Hasadiah, Jushabhesed, five. Next time you are caught inappropriately shouting, Oh Hell, just explain that you were calling out the name of the biblical figure Ohel - you know, the son of Zerubbabel. And the sons of Hananiah; Pelatiah, and Jesaiah: the sons of Rephaiah, the sons of Arnan, the sons of Obadiah, the sons of Shechaniah. And the sons of Shechaniah; Shemaiah: and the sons of Shemaiah; Hattush, and Igeal, and Bariah, and Neariah, and Shaphat, six. And the sons of Neariah; Elioenai, and Hezekiah, and Azrikam, three. And the sons of Elioenai were, Hodaiah, and Eliashib, and Pelaiah, and Akkub, and Johanan, and Dalaiah, and Anani, seven. The sons of Judah; Pharez, Hezron, and Carmi, and Hur, and Shobal. And Reaiah the son of Shobal begat Jahath; and Jahath begat Ahumai, and Lahad. These are the families of the Zorathites. And these were of the father of Etam; Jezreel, and Ishma, and Idbash: and the name of their sister was Hazelelponi: And Penuel the father of Gedor, and Ezer the father of Hushah. These are the sons of Hur, the firstborn of Ephratah, the father of Bethlehem. And Ashur the father of Tekoa had two wives, Helah and Naarah. And Naarah bare him Ahuzam, and Hepher, and Temeni, and Haahashtari. These were the sons of Naarah. And the sons of Helah were, Zereth, and Jezoar, and Ethnan. And Coz begat Anub, and Zobebah, and the families of Aharhel the son of Harum. And Jabez was more honorable than his brethren: and his mother called his name Jabez, saying, Because I bare him with sorrow. And Jabez called on the God of Israel, saying, Oh that thou wouldest bless me indeed, and enlarge my coast, and that thine hand might be with me, and that thou wouldest keep me from evil, that it may not grieve me! Oh and that thou wouldest enlarge my big screen tv, and while thou art at it enlarge my rv, that it may not grieve me by being a little too cramped next time I go camping with the wife and kids. And God granted him that which he requested. And Chelub the brother of Shuah begat Mehir, which was the father of Eshton. And Eshton begat Bethrapha, and Paseah, and Tehinnah the father of Irnahash. These are the men of Rechah. And the sons of Kenaz; Othniel, and Seraiah: and the sons of Othniel; Hathath. And Meonothai begat Ophrah: and Seraiah begat Joab, the father of the valley of Charashim; for they were craftsmen. And the sons of Caleb the son of Jephunneh; Iru, Elah, and Naam: and the sons of Elah, even Kenaz. And the sons of Jehaleleel; Ziph, and Ziphah, Tiria, and Asareel. And the sons of Ezra were, Jether, and Mered, and Epher, and Jalon: and she bare Miriam, and Shammai, and Ishbah the father of Eshtemoa. And his wife Jehudijah bare Jered the father of Gedor, and Heber the father of Socho, and Jekuthiel the father of Zanoah. And these are the sons of Bithiah the daughter of Pharaoh, which Mered took. And the sons of his wife Hodiah the sister of Naham, the father of Keilah the Garmite, and Eshtemoa the Maachathite. And the sons of Shimon were, Amnon, and Rinnah, Benhanan, and Tilon. And the sons of Ishi were, Zoheth, and Benzoheth. The sons of Shelah the son of Judah were, Er the father of Lecah, and Laadah the father of Mareshah, and the families of the house of them that wrought fine linen, of the house of Ashbea, And Jokim, and the men of Chozeba, and Joash, and Saraph, who had the dominion in Moab, and Jashubilehem. And these are ancient things. These were the potters,

and those that dwelt among plants and hedges: there they dwelt with the king for his work. The sons of Simeon were, Nemuel, and Jamin, Jarib, Zerah, and Shaul: Shallum his son, Mibsam his son, Mishma his son. And the sons of Mishma; Hamuel his son, Zacchur his son, Shimei his son. And Shimei had sixteen sons and six daughters; but his brethren had not many children, neither did all their family multiply, like to the children of Judah. And they dwelt at Beersheba, and Moladah, and Hazarshual, And at Bilhah, and at Ezem, and at Tolad, And at Bethuel, and at Hormah, and at Ziklag, And at Bethmarcaboth, and Hazarsusim, and at Bethbirei, and at Shaaraim. These were their cities unto the reign of David. And their villages were, Etam, and Ain, Rimmon, and Tochen, and Ashan, five cities: And all their villages that were round about the same cities, unto Baal. These were their habitations, and their genealogy. And Meshobab, and Jamlech, and Joshah, the son of Amaziah, And Joel, and Jehu the son of Josibiah, the son of Seraiah, the son of Asiel, And Elioenai, and Jaakobah, and Jeshohaiah, and Asaiah, and Adiel, and Jesimiel, and Benaiah, And Ziza the son of Shiphi, the son of Allon, the son of Jedaiah, the son of Shimri, the son of Shemaiah. Now keep reading because it's about to get really good: you'll learn about some really fat pastures, get down to the real business of smiting and causing general destruction, and then there's even more exciting pasture updates. Don't give up now! These mentioned by their names were princes in their families: and the house of their fathers increased greatly. And they went to the entrance of Gedor, even unto the east side of the valley, to seek pasture for their flocks. And they found fat pasture and good, and the land was wide, and quiet, and peaceable; for they of Ham had dwelt there of old. And these written by name came in the days of Hezekiah king of Judah, and smote their tents, and the habitations that were found there, and destroyed them utterly unto this day, and dwelt in their rooms: because there was pasture there for their flocks. And some of them, even of the sons of Simeon, five hundred men, went to mount Seir, having for their captains Pelatiah, and Neariah, and Rephaiah, and Uzziel, the sons of Ishi. And they smote the rest of the Amalekites that were escaped, and dwelt there unto this day. Now the sons of Reuben the firstborn of Israel, (for he was the firstborn; but, forasmuch as he defiled his father's bed, his birthright was given unto the sons of Joseph the son of Israel: and the genealogy is not to be reckoned after the birthright. For Judah prevailed above his brethren, and of him came the chief ruler; but the birthright was Joseph's:) The sons, I say, of Reuben the firstborn of Israel were, Hanoch, and Pallu, Hezron, and Carmi. The sons of Joel; Shemaiah his son, Gog his son, Shimei his son, Micah his son, Reaia his son, Baal his son, Beerah his son, whom Tilgathpilneser king of Assyria carried away captive: he was prince of the Reubenites. And his brethren by their families, when the genealogy of their generations was reckoned, were the chief, Jeiel, and Zechariah, And Bela the son of Azaz, the son of Shema, the son of Joel, who dwelt in Aroer, even unto Nebo and Baalmeon: And eastward he inhabited unto the entering in of the wilderness from the river Euphrates: because their cattle were multiplied in the land of Gilead. And in the days of Saul they made war with the Hagarites, who fell by their hand: and they dwelt in their tents throughout all the east land of Gilead. And the children of Gad dwelt over against them, in the land of Bashan unto Salcah: Joel the chief, and Shapham the next, and Jaanai, and Shaphat in Bashan. And their brethren of the house of their fathers were, Michael, and Meshullam, and Sheba, and Jorai, and Jachan, and Zia, and Heber, seven. These are the children of Abihail the son of Huri, the son of Jaroah, the son of Gilead, the son of Michael, the son of Jeshishai, the son of Jahdo, the son of Buz.

book of records of the Chronicles, and they were read before the king. *Esther 6:1*

PUBLIC POLICY

There are those who suggest that the Bible should be the primary source on which to base our laws and social policies. Even if you read it very carefully, you won't find Moses advocating for a representative form of government, King David urging universal suffrage, or Jesus recommending a complex system of checks and balances. Here are a few of the biblical ideas that stand in direct contrast to the standard laws and customs that exist in most developed countries.

And he that smiteth his father or his mother shall be surely put to death. And he that stealeth a man and selleth him, or if he be found in his hand, he shall surely be put to death. And he that **curseth his father or his mother** shall surely be put to death.

Exodus 21:15-17 📖 *Wouldn't this increase the rates of parental smiting, since you'll be just as dead when you curse them as when you smite them?*

THE UNTOLD STORY
The Deleted Details from Popular Passages

If men quarrel, and one **strike a woman with child**, and she miscarry indeed, but live herself, he shall be answerable for so much damage as the woman's husband shall require and as arbiters shall award. But if her death ensue thereupon, he shall render life for life.

Exodus 21:22-23 📖 *The Bible's ruling on the thorny issue of the unborn: the fetus has some unspecified value, but it doesn't have the value that the mother's life has. That should settle the issue once and for all!*

If the sun be risen upon him, there shall be blood shed for him, for he should make full restitution. If he have nothing, then he shall be **sold for his theft**.

Exodus 22:3 📖 *So if you don't want to be sold into slavery, only steal what you can pay back.*

And cuttings for a dead person shall ye not make in your flesh, **nor put any tattoo** writing upon you. I am Jehovah.

Leviticus 19:28 📖 *Anti-tattoo legislation may prove to be very popular with older voters.*

The daughter of any priest, if she profane herself by **playing the prostitute**, she profanes her father. She shall be burnt with fire.

Leviticus 21:9 📖 *This appears to be less of an issue in our day; otherwise, we would certainly be seeing the headline "Priest Kills Prostitute" on a more regular basis.*

Yahweh spoke to Moses, saying, "Speak to Aaron, saying, 'Whoever he be of your seed throughout their generations that has a blemish, let him not approach to offer the bread of his God. For whatever man he be that has a blemish, he shall not approach: **a blind man, or a lame, or he that has a flat nose**, or any deformity, or a man that is broken-footed, or broken-handed, or crook-backed, or a dwarf, or that has a blemish in his eye, or is scurvy, or scabbed, or has his stones broken. No man of the seed of Aaron the priest, that has a blemish, shall come near to offer the offerings of Yahweh made by fire. He has a blemish. He shall not come near to offer the bread of his God.'"

Leviticus 21:16-21 Priest position available: no flat-nosers need apply.

If feelings of jealousy come over her husband and he suspects his wife, then he is to take her to the priest. Then the priest is to have the woman drink the bitter water. If she has been unfaithful to her husband, then when she is made to drink the bitter water, it will go into her **causing disease of the stomach** and wasting of the legs. But if she is clean, she will be free and will have offspring.

Numbers 5:14,15,26-28 How many women got away with adultery by passing this test?

Thou shalt not bow down thyself unto them nor serve them, for I, Jehovah, thy God, am a jealous God, visiting the iniquity of the fathers upon the children, and **upon the third and upon the fourth generation** of them that hate me.

Deuteronomy 5:9 "Worship other gods, and I'll punish your great-grandchildren."

If a man have two wives, the one beloved, and the other hated, and they have borne him children, both the beloved and the hated, and if the first-born son be hers that was hated, then it shall be, in the day that he causeth his sons to inherit that which he hath, that he may not make the son of the beloved the first-born before the son of the hated, who is the first-born. But he shall acknowledge the first-born, the son of the hated, by giving him a double portion of all that he hath, for he is the beginning of his strength. The right of the first-born is his.

Deuteronomy 21:15-17 "Do I really have to give an inheritance to that son of a…?"

Then shall his father and his mother lay hold on him and bring him out unto the elders of his city and unto the gate of his place. And they shall say unto the elders of his city, "This our son is **stubborn and rebellious**. He will not obey our voice. He is a glutton and a drunkard." And all the men of his city shall stone him to death with stones. So shalt thou put away the evil from the midst of thee, and all Israel shall hear and fear.

Deuteronomy 21:18-21 "He's a glutton and a drunkard, and I think he might be getting stoned too."

JESUS' POLITICAL LEANINGS

To prove that Jesus would vote like you, just search the gospels! Here are a few clues to his political ideology.

The NOT-Stereotypically-Conservative Jesus

Jesus suggests that the rich go to hell for being rich. *Luke 16:25*
Jesus says don't defend yourself when you're attacked. *Matt. 5:39*
The overtly religious are worse than tax collectors. *Luke 18:14*
Jesus says if anyone steals from you, don't ask for it back. *Luke 6:30*
Jesus warns that we shouldn't pray in public. *Matt. 6:5*
Jesus says feed and clothe the least important people. *Matt. 25:45*
The poor should pay less to the treasury than the rich. *Luke 21:1-3*
"Sell everything you have and give it to the poor." *Luke 18:22*
Jesus requires his followers to not judge others. *Matt. 7:1*
Jesus doesn't believe in the inerrancy of the Bible. *Mark 10:5*
Jesus recommends against using swords. *Matt. 26:52*
Jesus casts out merchants from the temple. *Luke 19:45*

The NOT-Stereotypically-Liberal Jesus

Jesus says the rich will get richer and the poor poorer. *Mark 4:25*
Jesus warns about the necessity of a strong defense. *Luke 11:22*
Jesus recommends capital punishment. *Luke 20:16*
Jesus promotes high returns on investments. *Matt. 25:21*
Jesus says to sell your clothes and buy a sword." *Luke 22:36*
Ending poverty is secondary to worshiping Jesus. *John 12:8*
Jesus claims it's okay to judge, just not on appearances. *John 7:24*
Jesus is a biblical literalist when it comes to the flood. *Matt. 24:39*
"I came not to send peace, but a sword." *Matt. 10:34*
Jesus kills a tree that he disliked. *Matt. 21:19*
His father's house has many mansions. *John 14:2*

No man whose private parts have been wounded or cut off may come into the meeting of the Lord's people. One whose father and mother are not married may not come into the meeting of the Lord's people, or any of his family to the tenth generation.

> *Deuteronomy 23:1-2* "Welcome everyone to the Lord's People's Meeting. I'd like to welcome back after a long absence Bob, the great-great-great-great-great-great-great-great grandson of Joe the Bastard."

Do not take interest from an Israelite on anything: money, or food, or any other goods which you let him have. From men of other nations you may take interest, but not from an Israelite, so that the blessing of the Lord your God may be on everything to which you put your hand, in the land which you are about to take as your heritage.

> *Deuteronomy 23:19-20* So are Bible adherents around the globe allowed to charge Israelis interest?

And unto David were sons born in Hebron. And his first-born was Amnon, of Ahinoam the Jezreelitess, and his second, Chileab, of Abigail the wife of Nabal the Carmelite, and the third, Absalom the son of Maacah, the daughter of Talmai, king of Geshur, and the fourth, Adonijah the son of Haggith, and the fifth, Shephatiah the son of Abital, and the sixth, Ithream, of Eglah, David's wife. These were born to David in Hebron.

> *2 Samuel 3:2-5* Six wives, six children: good parent-to-child ratios make child rearing easier.

For David had offered that day a reward to whosoever should strike the Jebusites, and get up to the gutters of the tops of the houses, and take away the blind and the lame that hated the soul of David. Therefore it is said in the proverb: *The blind and the lame shall not come into the temple*.

> *2 Samuel 5:8* This proverb conflicts with a more recent proverb: "ADA compliant."

Now King Solomon loved many foreign women, together with the daughter of Pharaoh, women of the Moabites, Ammonites, Edomites, Sidonians, and Hittites, of the nations concerning which Jehovah said unto the children of Israel, "Ye shall not go among them, neither shall they come among you, for surely they will turn away your heart after their gods." Solomon clave unto these in love. *And he had seven hundred wives, princesses, and three hundred concubines*, and his wives turned away his heart.

> *1 Kings 11:1-3* "I'm tired of being concubine #207! When are you going to make me wife #701?"

Rehoboam loved Maacah the daughter of Absalom **above all his wives and his concubines** (for he took eighteen wives and sixty concubines, and he became the father of twenty-eight sons and sixty daughters.)

2 Chronicles 11:21 ⚱ *I bet he told that to all his wives and concubines.*

NEVER ON A **SUNDAY** SCHOOL'S READING LIST

But Abijah grew powerful in his kingdom, and **took to himself fourteen wives**, and became the father of twenty-two sons and sixteen daughters.

2 Chronicles 13:21 ⚱ *"If only we could stone rebellious sons. That could help keep a high female-to-male ratio and more wives for me!"*

The Lord hath said to me, "Thou art my son. This day have I begotten thee. Ask of me, and I will give thee the Gentiles for thy inheritance and the utmost parts of the earth for thy possession. Thou shalt **rule them with a rod of iron** and shalt break them in pieces like a potter's vessel."

Psalms 2:7-9 ⚱ *Doesn't this passage have all the makings of a chart-topping church hymn? Just listen to the choir piously belt it out next time Handel's* Messiah *is performed near you.*

Let Samaria perish, because she hath stirred up her God to bitterness. Let them perish by the sword. Let their little ones be dashed, and **let the women with child be ripped up**.

WHOLLY UNHOLY
The Dark Side of the Bible

Hosea 13:16 ⚱ *Let's all agree to rewrite this verse to read "let the women with child go free."*

Saying to them, "Go into the village over against you, and immediately ye shall find an ass tied and a colt with her. Loose them, and **bring them to me**."

Matthew 21:2 ⚱ *"On Jesus' orders you're taking my colt, my ass! Who died and made him emperor?"*

THE AWFULLY UNLAWFUL BIBLE

"But, officer, it says right here in Leviticus 21:9..."

⚱ The following passages would appear to explicitly or implicitly condone activities that are illegal or are considered unacceptable in most countries throughout the world.

Slavery
Exodus 21:1-11 etc.

Tattoo prohibition
Leviticus 19:28

Burning a prostitute
Leviticus 21:9

Discriminating against the blind, handicapped, flat-nosed, blemished, scabbed, and dwarves
Leviticus 21:16-21

Stoning for working on the Sabbath
Numbers 15:32-36

Punishing a child for a parent's sin
Deuteronomy 5:9

Religiously-selective favoritism in business practices
Deuteronomy 23:20-21

Stoning a stubborn son
Deuteronomy 21:18-21

Stoning for falsely claiming to be a virgin
Deuteronomy 22:20-21

Discriminating against the genitally wounded
Deuteronomy 23:2

Remarrying your first husband prohibition
Deuteronomy 24:1-4

Polygamy
2 Samuel 3:2-5; 1 Kings 11:1-3 etc.

No freedom of religion
2 Kings 10:25

Massive animal sacrifice
2 Chronicles 7:5

Oxicide equal to homicide
Isaiah 66:3

War crimes (e.g., killing infants and pregnant women)
Hosea 13:16; 1 Samuel 15:3

Discrimination against women
1 Timothy 2:11-15

SABBATH

Before modern labor laws, having a forced vacation once a week must have sounded very appealing. That is, until you learned that being a little too active on that day meant that you got a visit from all your neighbors who lived just a stone's throw away.

Ye shall keep the sabbath therefore, for it is holy unto you. Every one that profaneth it shall **surely be put to death**. For whosoever doeth any work therein, that soul shall be cut off from among his people. Six days shall work be done, but on the seventh day is a sabbath of solemn rest, holy to Jehovah. Whosoever doeth any work on the sabbath day, he shall surely be put to death.

Exodus 31:14-15 ⚰ *Nothing proves how holy your sabbath is like a good old-fashioned stoning.*

WHOLLY UNHOLY
The Dark Side of the Bible

And while the children of Israel were in the wilderness, they found a man *gathering sticks upon the sabbath day*. And they that found him gathering sticks brought him unto Moses and Aaron, and unto all the congregation. And they put him in ward, because it had not been declared what should be done to him. And Jehovah said unto Moses, "The man shall surely be put to death. All the congregation shall stone him with stones without the camp." And all the congregation brought him without the camp and stoned him to death with stones as Jehovah commanded Moses.

Numbers 15:32-36 ⚰ *Sticks and stones may break your bones!*

Or have ye not read in the law, how that on the sabbath days the priests in the temple **profane the sabbath** and are blameless?

Matthew 12:5 ⚰ *Jesus cites a law that's not found in the Bible, but as it says in the law, when you make up a Bible reference, you are blameless.*

For this reason **let no man be your judge** in any question of food, or drink, or feast days, or new moons, or Sabbaths.

Colossians 2:16 ⚰ *"Don't tell me tomorrow's not a new moon."*

SEX

When Jehovah was just starting out, he had to compete against many other religions, some of which offered their followers sex rituals performed by prostitutes at their shrines. Of course, Jehovah's idea of competing was to command the destruction of those shrines which contained "abominable" carvings, thus explaining Jehovah's dislike of graven images and prostitution. Often left unpreached are the following steamy and shocking Bible verses about sex which somehow found their way into the Holy Scriptures.

Now Sarai, Abram's wife, had given him no children, and she had a servant, a woman of Egypt whose name was Hagar. And Sarai said to Abram, "See, the Lord has not let me have children. **Go in to my servant**, for I may get a family through her." And Abram did as Sarai said. So after Abram had been living for ten years in the land of Canaan, Sarai took Hagar, her Egyptian servant, and gave her to Abram for his wife. And he went in to Hagar and she became with child, and when she saw that she was with child, she no longer had any respect for her master's wife. And Sarai said to Abram, "May my wrong be on you. I gave you my servant for your wife, and when she saw that she was with child, she no longer had any respect for me. May the Lord be judge between you and me." And Abram said, "The woman is in your power. Do with her whatever seems good to you." And Sarai was cruel to her, so that she went running away from her.

Genesis 16:1-6 📖 *As true then as it is now, it's hard to find good help.*

But before they had gone to bed, the men of the town, all the men of Sodom, came round the house, young and old, from every part of the town. And crying out to Lot, they said, "Where are the men who came to your house this night? Send them out to us, so that we may take our pleasure with them." And Lot went out to them in the doorway, shutting the door after him. And he said, "My brothers, do not this evil. See now, **I have two unmarried daughters**. I will send them out to you so that you may do to them whatever seems good to you. Only do nothing to these men, for this is why they have come under the shade of my roof."

Genesis 19:4-8 📖 *And the moral of the story is that it really is best to try to be born male.*

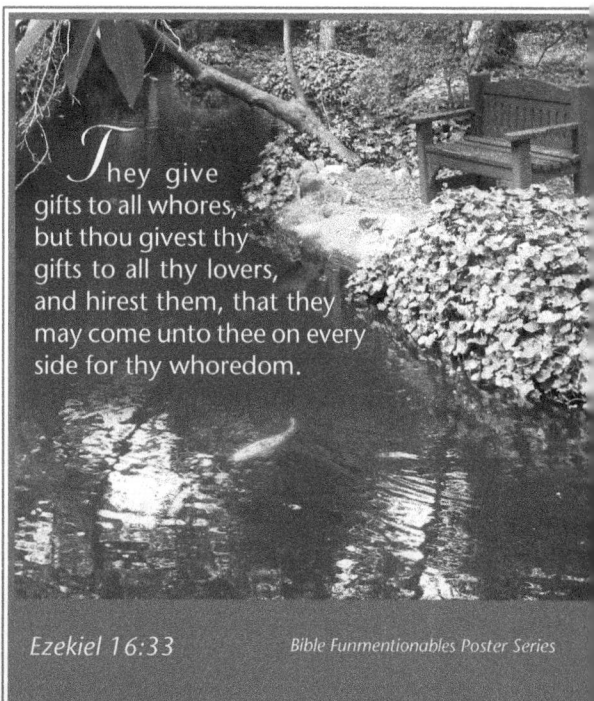

*T*hey give gifts to all whores, but thou givest thy gifts to all thy lovers, and hirest them, that they may come unto thee on every side for thy whoredom.

Ezekiel 16:33   Bible Funmentionables Poster Series

PITY THE TRANSLATOR 1

Your assignment: come up with a pleasant phrase to describe a defiling dream a man might have which would make him have to wash up afterwards. Below is the Douay-Rheims translation followed by alternate translations.

" If there be among you any man that is **defiled in a dream by night**, he shall go forth out of the camp and shall not return before he be washed with water in the evening, and after sunset he shall return into the camp.
Deuteronomy 23:10-11

If there be among you any man, that is not clean...

• by reason of **that which chanceth him by night**
American Standard Version

• by reason of **uncleanness that chanceth to him by night**
Webster's

• from **an accident at night**
Young's Literal Translation

• by reason of **uncleanness that chanceth him by night**
King James Version

• from **what hath happened in the night**
Darby Translation

• by reason of **that which happens him by night**
World English Bible

• through **anything which has taken place in the night**
Bible in Basic English

Then Lot went up out of Zoar to the mountain and was living there with his two daughters, for fear kept him from living in Zoar. And he and his daughters made their living-place in a hole in the rock. And the older daughter said to her sister, "Our father is old, and there is no man to be a husband to us in the natural way. Come, **let us give our father much wine, and we will go into his bed**, so that we may have offspring by our father." And that night they made their father take much wine, and the older daughter went into his bed, and he had no knowledge of when she went in or when she went away. And on the day after, the older daughter said to the younger, "Last night I was with my father. Let us make him take much wine this night again, and do you go to him, so that we may have offspring by our father." And that night again they made their father take much wine, and the younger daughter went into his bed, and he had no knowledge of when she went in or when she went away. And so the two daughters of Lot were with child by their father.
Genesis 19:30-36 Cave life ain't easy.

A PRAYER for Eating Fruit or for Being Fruitful & Multiplying?

Read the following verse as a stern preacher might and then again with a knowing, breathless intonation, and you'll see how much the Bible is open to interpretation.

" Awake, O north wind, and come, thou south. Blow upon my garden, that the spices thereof may flow out. Let my beloved come into his garden and eat his pleasant fruits. *Song of Songs 4:16*

Now Rachel, because she had no children, was full of envy of her sister, and she said to Jacob, "If you do not give me children I will not go on living." But Jacob was angry with Rachel and said, "Am I in the place of God, who has kept your body from having fruit?" Then she said, "Here is my servant Bilhah, *go in to her, so that she may have a child on my knees*, and I may have a family by her." So she gave him her servant Bilhah as a wife, and Jacob went in to her. And Bilhah became with child and gave birth to a son. Then Rachel said, "God has been my judge, and has given ear to my voice, and has given me a son, so he was named Dan."

Genesis 30:1-6 ⚰ *Another episode of* The Old and the Childless.

Now at the time of the grain-cutting, Reuben saw some love-fruits in the field and took them to his mother Leah. And Rachel said to Leah, "Let me have some of your son's love-fruits." But Leah said to her, "Is it a small thing that you have taken my husband Jacob from me? And now would you take my son's love-fruits?" Then Rachel said, "*You may have Jacob tonight in exchange for your son's love-fruits*." In the evening, when Jacob came in from the field, Leah went out to him and said, "Tonight you are to come to me, for I have given my son's love-fruits as a price for you." And he went in to her that night. And God gave ear to her, and she became with child, and gave Jacob a fifth son. Then Leah said, "God has made payment to me for giving my servant-girl to my husband." So she gave her son the name Issachar.

Genesis 30:14-18 ⚰ *Here's a good way to teach children the ancient practice of bartering.*

And he said, "Who are you?" And she answered, "I am Ruth, thy servant. *Spread therefore thy skirt over thy servant* for you are a near relation."

Ruth 3:9 ⚰ *Servant skirt spreading alliteratively alludes to amorous adult activities.*

UNSAFE PASSAGE Unsuitable for Student-Led Prayer

THE BIBLE'S SEXUAL FREQUENCY

BIBLE FUNMENTIONABLE QUIZ

What was on the minds of the Bible's authors regarding all matters sexual? Match the word below with the number of times it appears in the Bible immediately following the word "sexual."

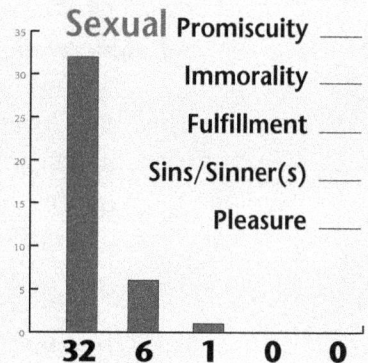

Sexual Promiscuity ___
Immorality ___
Fulfillment ___
Sins/Sinner(s) ___
Pleasure ___

32 6 1 0 0

According to the World English Bible translation, first place goes to Sexual Immorality with 32 occurrences, followed by Sin/Sinner(s) with 6, and Promiscuity with 1. Sexual fulfillment and pleasure are evidently not so important.

Those used for sex purposes in the worship of the gods he sent out of the country, and he took away all the images which his fathers had made. And he would not let Maacah his mother be queen, because she had made *a disgusting image for Asherah*, and Asa had the image cut down and burned by the stream Kidron.

1 Kings 15:12-13 ⚰ *It's a fallacy that these disgusting carved wooden poles to the fertility goddess Asherah didn't get the authors of the Bible all hot and bothered.*

Now King David was old and stricken in years, and though they covered him with clothes, his body was cold. Therefore his servants said to him, "Let there be sought for my lord the king a young virgin, and let her stand before the king and cherish him. And **let her lie in your bosom**, that my lord the king may keep warm." So they sought a beautiful young lady throughout all the borders of Israel, and found Abishag the Shunammite, and brought her to the king. The young lady was very beautiful, and she cherished the king and ministered to him, but the king didn't know her intimately.

1 Kings 1:1-4 📖 How many subsequent kings used the "No, I'm still cold" ruse in order to procure their own virgins? If the Bible recommends a beautiful young lady over my electric blanket, thy will be done.

UNLIKELY SIGN
From a Fan in the Stands
PROVERBS 5:19
Rapturous Breasts!

Let blessing be on your fountain. Have joy in the wife of your early years. As a loving hind and a gentle doe, **let her breasts ever give you rapture**. Let your passion at all times be moved by her love.

Proverbs 5:18-19 📖 Lovely sentiments—and blessed be your fountain!

So I came out in the hope of meeting you, looking for you with care, and now I have you. My bed is covered with cushions of needlework, with colored cloths of the cotton thread of Egypt. I have made my bed sweet with perfumes and spices. Come, let us take our pleasure in love till the morning, having joy in love's delights, for the master of the house is away on a long journey. He has taken a bag of money with him. He is coming back at the full moon. **With her fair words she overcame him, forcing him with her smooth lips**. The simple man goes after her, like an ox going to its death, like a roe pulled by a cord, like a bird falling into a net, with no thought that his life is in danger, till an arrow goes into his side.

Proverbs 7:15-23 📖 You had me until you used your ox death analogy.

Thy two breasts are like two fawns, twins of a gazelle, which feed among the lilies.

Song of Songs 4:5 📖 Was I sick the day we discussed this in religion class?

My beloved **put in his hand by the hole** of the door, and my heart was moved for him.

Song of Songs 5:4 📖 Verses that make little sense when taken literally require a more symbolic interpretation.

This thy stature is like to a palm tree, and **thy breasts to clusters of grapes**.

Song of Songs 7:7 📖 This certainly is a contender to top the list of ineffective biblical pick-up lines.

"I caused thee to multiply as the bud of the field, and you were increased and became great. And you came to the time of love. **Your breasts were formed and your hair was long**, but you were uncovered and without clothing. Now when I went past you, looking at you, I saw that your time was the time of love, and I put my skirts over you, covering your un-clothed body. And I gave you my oath and made an agreement with you," says the Lord, "and you became mine."

Ezekiel 16:7-8 ⚰ *Uncharacteristically suggestive for holy scripture.*

A drunken woman is a great wrath, and her reproach and shame shall not be hid. The fornication of a woman shall be known by the haughtiness of her eyes, and by her eyelids. On a daughter that turneth not away herself, set a strict watch, lest finding an opportunity she abuse herself.

Sirach 26:11-13

Bible Funmentionables Poster Series

But still she went on the more with her loose behavior, keeping in mind the early days when she had been a loose woman in the land of Egypt. And she was full of desire for her lovers, **whose flesh is like the flesh of asses** and whose seed is like the seed of horses. And she made the memory of the loose ways of her early years come back to mind, when her young breasts were crushed by the Egyptians.

Ezekiel 23:19-21 ⚰ *One Bible mystery that still divides theologians: did they con-sider it a positive or negative thing to have the flesh of asses?*

UNSAFE PASSAGE
Unsuitable for Student-Led Prayer

BIBLE FUNMENTIONABLES QUIZ
THAT WHICH SHALL NOT BE NAMED

The authors of the Bible were thoughtful enough to use euphemisms for potentially embarrassing terms. The words below are grouped by their euphemistic meaning. Try to spot the one impostor in each group.

Group 1
HE/SHE approached
came in unto
came at
carried a package
defiled
discovered his skirt
duty of marriage
ground unto
humbled
knew
lay carnally
lay down with

lay with
loved
obtained children by
played the harlot
spread your skirt over
slept with
touched
uncovered nakedness
visited
was sporting with
went in to
went in unto
went up to his couch

Group 2
HIS feet
flesh
grain-cutter
horn
loins
mandrakes
manhood
member
navel
secrets
tail
thigh

Group 3
HER beauty
feet
peculiar treasure
place of the
    breaking forth
    of children
secret parts
uncomely parts

Group 4
HE/SHE breathed his last
fell asleep
lamp went out
sailed away
slept with his fathers
returned to the ground
was gathered to his people
went down to the grave

According to current scholarly consensus: in Group 1: "carried a package" didn't refer to sexual intercourse; in Group 2: "grain-cutter" didn't refer to male genitalia; in Group 3: "peculiar treasure" didn't refer to female genitalia; in Group 4: "sailed away" didn't refer to death.

WOMEN

If there is one topic that demonstrates that the Bible was written in a time and place much different from our own, it is the role of women in society. See if you can tell which of the following Bible passages were written by men.

To the woman he said, "I will greatly increase thy travail and thy pregnancy. With pain thou shalt bear children, and to thy husband shall be thy desire, and he shall **rule over thee**.
Genesis 3:16 🕮 *Eve ate some fruit; so logically, husbands should rule over their wives ever after.*

Passage of Questionable Relevance

And if a man entice a virgin that is not betrothed, and lie with her, he shall surely pay a dowry for her to be his wife. If her father utterly refuse to give her unto him, he shall pay money according to the dowry of virgins.
Exodus 22:16-17 🕮 *Guys, be sure to ask your girlfriend's parents when you're first dating, "What is the going rate for a virgin's dowry these days?"*

But if what he has said is true, and **she is seen to be not a virgin**, then they are to make the girl come to the door of her father's house, and she will be stoned to death by the men of the town, because she has done evil and put shame on Israel by acting as a loose woman in her father's house. So you are to put away evil from among you.
Deuteronomy 22:20-21 🕮 *The Bible is oddly silent on the issue of a man who turns out not to be a virgin.*

If a man takes a wife, and after they are married **she is unpleasing to him** because of some bad quality in her, let him give her a statement in writing and send her away from his house. And when she has gone away from him, she may become another man's wife. And if the second husband has no love for her and, giving her a statement in writing, sends her away, or if death comes to the second husband to whom she was married, her first husband, who had sent her away, may not take her back after she has been wife to another, for that is disgusting to the Lord. And you are not to be a cause of sin in the land which the Lord your God is giving you for your heritage.
Deuteronomy 24:1-4 🕮 *Known to theologians as the "No Take-backs" rule.*

If brethren dwell together, and one of them die and have no son, the wife of the dead shall not marry a stranger abroad. **Her husband's brother shall go in unto her**, and take her to him as wife, and perform the duty of a husband's brother unto her.

Deuteronomy 25:5 ⚱ I saw this in a Bible movie once...I think it was called Hamlet.

And Abimelech came to the tower, and made an attack on it, and got near to the door of the tower for the purpose of firing it. But a certain woman sent a great stone, such as is used for crushing grain, onto the head of Abimelech, cracking the bone. Then quickly crying out to his body-servant, he said to him, "Take out your sword and put an end to me straight away, so that men may not say of me, '**His death was the work of a woman**.'" So the young man put his sword through him, causing his death.

Judges 9:52-54 ⚱ "I toss this grain-crushing stone for all those women out there who never got to join in those public stonings."

And they commanded the children of Benjamin and said, "Go and lie hid in the vineyards, and when you shall see the **daughters of Silo** come out, as the custom is, to dance, come ye on a sudden out of the vineyards, and catch you every man his wife among them, and go into the land of Benjamin."

Judges 21:20-21 ⚱ They only resorted to this when their recent killing spree in Jabeshgilead netted them only 400 virgins.

PITY THE TRANSLATOR 2

Some of the more colorful Bible phrases have to be translated delicately to avoid upsetting the faithful through the ages. Below is a sample of how a few translators struggled with that challenge.

Now Rachel had taken the idols and put them inside her camel's saddle and sat on them. Laban searched the whole tent but did not find them. Rachel said to her father, "Don't be angry, my lord. I cannot stand up in your presence because **I am having my period**." So he searched thoroughly, but did not find the idols.
Genesis 31:34-35

I am not able to rise at thy presence, for **the way of women is on me**.
Young's Literal Translation

I cannot rise up before thee, because **it has now happened to me, according to the custom of women**.
Douay-Rheims

I cannot rise up before thee, for **the custom of women is upon me**.
King James Version

I cannot rise before you, for **I am in the common condition of women**.
Bible in Basic English

And the prize for the Most Unintelligible Translation:

I cannot rise up before thee, for **it is with me after the manner of women**.
Darby Translation

Moreover, Ruth the Moabitess, the wife of Mahlon, have **I purchased to be my wife**, to raise up the name of the dead upon his inheritance, that the name of the dead be not cut off from among his brethren, and from the gate of his place. Ye are witnesses this day.

Ruth 4:10 📖 *Who knew that buying a wife could sound like such a noble endeavor?*

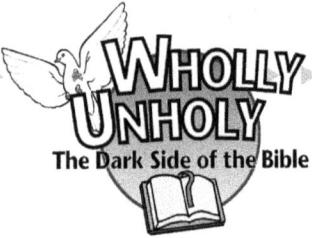

WHOLLY UNHOLY
The Dark Side of the Bible

Thus saith the Lord, "Behold, I will raise up evil against thee out of thine own house, and I will take thy wives before thine eyes and give them unto thy neighbor, and **he shall lie with thy wives** in the sight of this sun."

2 Samuel 12:11 📖 *God didn't actually hand David's wives over to his neighbors to be raped. He just threatened to do that.*

📖 **Bible Funmentionables' Guide to**

THE FOUR TYPES OF WOMEN TO AVOID

Like a ring of gold in **the nose of a pig** is a beautiful woman who has no sense.

Proverbs 11:22

It is better to dwell in **the corner of the housetop** than to share a house with a contentious woman.

Proverbs 21:9

It is better to **dwell in the wilderness** than with a contentious and an angry woman.

Proverbs 21:19

It is better to dwell in **the corner of the housetop** than to share a house with a contentious woman.

Proverbs 25:24

A continual dropping on a very rainy day and a contentious woman are alike.

Proverbs 27:15

And there is no anger above the anger of a woman. It will be more agreeable to **abide with a lion and a dragon** than to dwell with a wicked woman.

Sirach 25:23 📖 *Yeah, we're talking to you, angry, wicked, contentious, and senseless (though beautiful) women!*

Then Menahem smote Tiphsah, and all that were therein, and the borders thereof from Tirzah, because they opened not to him. Therefore he smote it, and **all the women therein that were with child** he ripped up.

2 Kings 15:16 📖 *You know you've been reading the Bible fairly thoroughly, when you come across the phrase "with child," and you find yourself desperately hoping it is not soon followed by the phrase "ripped up."*

Such is the way of an adulterous woman: she eateth, and **wipeth her mouth**, and saith, "I have done no wickedness."

Proverbs 30:20 📖 *So every woman who has wiped her mouth, yet claims to be innocent is obviously guilty.*

Zion spreadeth forth her hands, and there is none to comfort her. The Lord hath commanded concerning Jacob that his adversaries should be round about him. Jerusalem is as a **menstruous woman** among them.

Lamentations 1:17 📖 *You don't need a theology degree to know the gender of this verse's author.*

From the woman came **the beginning of sin**, and by her we all die.

Sirach 25:33 📖 *Responsible for death and sin. Way to go, women.*

But I would have you know, that the head of every man is Christ, and the head of the woman is the man, and the head of Christ is God. Every man praying or prophesying, having his head covered, dishonors his head. But every woman praying or prophesying with her head unveiled dishonors her head. For it is one and the same thing as if she were shaved. For if a woman is not covered, **let her also be shorn**. But if it is shameful for a woman to be shorn or shaved, let her be covered. For a man indeed ought not to have his head covered, because he is the image and glory of God, but the woman is the glory of the man. For man is not from woman, but woman from man. For neither was man created for the woman, but woman for the man. For this cause the woman ought to have authority on her head, because of the angels.

UNSAFE PASSAGE
Unsuitable for Student-Led Prayer

1 Corinthians 11:3-10 📖 *It's so simple. A woman should be veiled. If she's not veiled, she should be shorn. But she shouldn't be shorn, so she should be veiled. Because of the angels.*

BIBLE FUNMENTIONABLE! QUIZ

MEN VS. WOMEN: A BIBLICAL PERSPECTIVE

What better source for teaching gender roles to today's youth than a millennia-old, Middle Eastern collection of writings. Fill in the blanks below with either **MAN** or **WOMAN**.

To take a handful of the sacrifice of that which is offered, and burn it upon the altar, and so give the most bitter waters to the _____ to drink. *–Numbers 5:26*

That thou mayst keep thoughts, and thy lips may preserve instruction. Mind not the deceit of a _____. *–Proverbs 5:2*

For the price of a harlot is scarce one loaf, but the _____ catcheth the precious soul of a man. *–Proverbs 6:26*

The mouth of a strange _____ is a deep pit. He whom the Lord is angry with shall fall into it. *–Proverbs 22:14*

Now concerning the thing whereof you wrote to me: It is good for a man not to touch a _____. *–1 Corinthians 7:1*

The wickedness of a _____ changeth her face, and she darkeneth her countenance as a bear and showeth it like sackcloth in the midst of her neighbors. *–Sirach 25:24*

Feeble hands and disjointed knees, a _____ that doth not make her husband happy. *–Sirach 25:32*

A drunken _____ is a great wrath, and her reproach and shame shall not be hid. *–Sirach 26:11*

A holy and shamefaced _____ is grace upon grace. *–Sirach 26:19*

For better is the iniquity of a man, than a _____ doing a good turn, and a _____ bringing shame and reproach. *–Sirach 42:14*

ANSWER: *Maybe not surprisingly, the answer to all of the above is "woman."*

TOP TEN
The Best of the Worst

Let the **women keep silence in the churches**, for it is not permitted unto them to speak. But let them be in subjection, as also saith the law. And if they would learn anything, let them ask their own husbands at home, for it is shameful for a woman to speak in the church. What? Was it from you that the word of God went forth? Or came it unto you alone? If any man thinketh himself to be a prophet, or spiritual, let him take knowledge of the things which I write unto you, that they are the commandment of the Lord. But if any man is ignorant, let him be ignorant.

1 Corinthians 14:34-38 📖 *Yep, somebody sounds ignorant all right. And he might just have control issues too.*

Let women be subject to their husbands, as to the Lord, because the husband is the head of the wife, as Christ is the head of the church. He is the savior of his body. Therefore as the church is subject to Christ, so also let the wives be to their husbands in all things.

Ephesians 5:22-24 📖 *Makes perfect sense . . . especially to men.*

Nevertheless let every one of you in particular love his wife as himself, and **let the wife fear her husband**.

Ephesians 5:33 📖 *"I love you, honey." "And I fear you, darling."*

In like manner, that women adorn themselves in modest apparel, with shamefastness and sobriety, **not with braided hair**, and gold or pearls or costly attire.

1 Timothy 2:9 📖 *St. Paul didn't like women dressing up. He didn't like women speaking up. He didn't like women to be touched. And you wonder why a guy like him never married.*

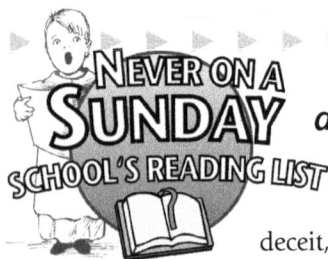

NEVER ON A SUNDAY
SCHOOL'S READING LIST

Let a woman quietly take the place of a learner and be under authority. In my opinion, **it is right for a woman not to be a teacher**, or to have rule over a man, but to be quiet. For Adam was first formed, then Eve. And Adam was not taken by deceit, but the woman, being tricked, became a wrongdoer. But if they go on in faith and love and holy self-control, she will be kept safe at the time of childbirth.

1 Timothy 2:11-15 📖 *I hope there are no women teachers out there.*

Wives, be ruled by your husbands, so that even if some of them give no attention to the word, their hearts may be changed by the behavior of their wives.

1 Peter 3:1 📖 *The best way to affect your husband's behavior is to do whatever he says without question.*

Behold, *I will throw her into a bed*, and those who commit adultery with her into great oppression, unless they repent of her works.

Revelation 2:22 📖 *Couldn't they just claim it was entrapment?*

Simon Peter said unto them, "Mary should leave from among us, since *females are not worthy of life*." Jesus said, "Look, I myself shall guide her so as to make her male, that she also may become a living spirit just as you males are. For every female who becomes male will enter the kingdom of heaven."

Gospel of Thomas #114 📖 *Wouldn't it have been easier to just answer, "You're wrong. They are worthy of life."*

📖 WHEN TO OFFER A WIDOW HELP

You can't in good conscience go around helping just any widow. According to 1 Timothy 5:9-16, there are widows that deserve help, and then there's the rest of them.

HELP A WIDOW WHO HAS
• Reached 60 years of age
• Married only once
• Earned a good reputation
• Raised children
• Been kind to strangers
• Washed the saints' feet
• Helped those in trouble
• Diligently done good deeds

DON'T HELP A WIDOW WHO IS
• Younger than 60
• Interested in marriage
• Idle
• A gossiper and a busybody

📖 AND SHE BARE (MOST LIKELY) A SON

Leviticus 12:2-5 tells us that the proud new mother of a girl is twice as unclean as the mother of a baby boy, but how much more noteworthy was a boy's birth in the Bible?

"She conceived and bare a son" appears **22** times.

"She conceived and bare a daughter" appears **2** times.

Wives, submit yourselves to your own husbands, as it is fit in the Lord.

Colossians 3:18   *Bible Funmentionables Poster Series*

ANIMALS

It is apparent that animals were a very important part of the lives of the ancients, because they appear so frequently throughout the Bible. Mostly you learn how to sacrifice animals, when to sacrifice them, who is to sacrifice them, why you should sacrifice them, how many of them to sacrifice, and lastly, that they thought bats were birds.

If a man opens a pit, or if a man digs a pit and doesn't cover it, and **a bull or a donkey falls into it**, the owner of the pit shall make it good. He shall give money to its owner, and the dead animal shall be his.

Exodus 21:33-34 🕮 *There's a name for people who have donkeys falling into their uncovered pits.*

UNSAFE PASSAGE
Unsuitable for Student-Led Prayer

If his offering to Yahweh is a burnt offering of birds, then he shall offer his offering of turtle-doves or of young pigeons. The priest shall bring it to the altar, and **wring off its head**, and burn it on the altar, and its blood shall be drained out on the side of the altar. And he shall take away its crop with its filth and cast it beside the altar on the east part, in the place of the ashes. And he shall tear it by its wings, but shall not divide it apart. The priest shall burn it on the altar, on the wood that is on the fire. It is a burnt offering, an offering made by fire, of a sweet savor to Yahweh.

Leviticus 1:14-17 🕮 *Who wouldn't love the sweet smell of burning, headless turtle-doves?*

And if ye walk contrary unto me and will not hearken unto me, I will bring seven times more plagues upon you according to your sins. And I will send the beast of the field among you, which shall **rob you of your children**, and destroy your cattle, and make you few in number, and your ways shall become desolate.

Leviticus 26:21-22 🕮 *Septuple plagues, infanticide, bovicide! As they say about omnipotence, if you've got it, flaunt it.*

And the Lord sent **fiery serpents** among the people, and they bit the people, and many people of Israel died.

Numbers 21:6 🕮 *But on the other hand, many people probably lived to proudly tell the tale about the time they saw all these fiery serpents totally attacking a bunch of people.*

And the Lord said, "I will destroy man, whom I have created, from the face of the earth — both man and beast, and the creeping thing, and the fowls of the air. I am sorry that I have made them."

Genesis 6:7 🐾 *God feels compelled to wipe out almost all of his creation after only ten generations (1,656 years), yet he also gets credit for being an intelligent designer.*

BIBLE FUNMENTIONABLES QUIZ

ALL CREATURES GREAT & SMALL (AND FICTIONAL)

For many of us, the only animals we were taught about from the Bible were those in Noah's ark and Daniel's lions' den. But depending on your translation, the Bible is full of all sorts of odd animals. Fill in the blanks below with either **DRAGON, MOUSE, OSTRICH,** or **UNICORN**.

1 And the _____ shall go down with them, and the bulls with the mighty. Their land shall be soaked with blood, and their ground with the fat of fat ones. *–Isaiah 34:7*

2 Praise the Lord from the earth, ye_____. *–Psalms 148:7*

3 Foxes will make their holes there, and it will be a meeting-place for _____. *–Isaiah 34:13*

4 And the wild asses stood upon the rocks, they snuffed up the wind like _____. *–Jeremiah 14:6*

5 They that did eat swine's flesh, and the abomination, and the _____: they shall be consumed together, saith the Lord. *–Isaiah 66:17*

6 Save me from the lion's mouth, and my lowness from the horns of the _____. *–Psalms 22:21*

7 And he built his sanctuary as of _____, in the land which he founded forever. *–Psalms 78:69*

8 Therefore shall _____ dwell there with the fig fauns. *–Jeremiah 50:39*

9 The beasts of the field will give me honor, the jackals and the _____. *–Isaiah 43:20*

10 And shall reduce them to pieces, as a calf of Libanus, and as the beloved son of _____. *–Psalms 29:6*

11 Thou shalt trample under foot the lion and the _____. *–Psalms 91:13*

12 Their wine is the poison of _____. *–Deuteronomy 32:33*

13 These also shall be reckoned among unclean things, of all that move upon the earth, the weasel, and the _____. *–Leviticus 11:29*

14 I have become a brother to the jackals, and go about in the company of _____. *–Job 30:29*

15 Is the wing of the _____ feeble, or is it because she has no feathers. *–Job 39:16*

Ostrich(es):3,9,14,15; Unicorn(s):1,6,7,10

Dragon(s):2,4,8,11,12; Mouse:5,13;

God brought him forth out of Egypt. He hath as it were **the strength of a unicorn**. He shall eat up the nations that are his enemies, and shall break their bones, and pierce them through with his arrows.

Numbers 24:8 📖 *God may want to try arrow piercing and bone breaking first, and then proceed to eating.*

If by chance you see a place which a bird has made for itself in a tree or on the earth, with young ones or eggs, and the mother bird seated on the young ones or on the eggs, do not take the mother bird with the young. See that you let the mother bird go, but **the young ones you may take**, so it will be well for you, and your life will be long.

Deuteronomy 22:6-7 📖 *Where would the egg industry be without this sound, though seemingly heartless, advice.*

Thou shalt not plow with an ox and an ass together.

Deuteronomy 22:10 📖 *Unless I'm not looking deeply enough into this passage, the spiritual implications appear to be superseded by the agricultural implications.*

Then went Samson down, and his father and his mother, to Timnah, and came to the vineyards of Timnah. And, behold, a young lion roared against him. And the Spirit of Jehovah came mightily upon him, and he rent him as he would have rent a kid. And he had nothing in his hand, but he told not his father or his mother what he had done. And he went down, and talked with the woman, and she pleased Samson well. And after a while he returned to take her, and he turned aside to see the carcass of the lion. And, behold, there was **a swarm of bees in the body of the lion**, and honey. And he took it into his hands and went on, eating as he went. And he came to his father and mother and gave unto them, and they did eat. But he told them not that he had taken the honey out of the body of the lion.

Judges 14:5-9 📖 *"We have a surprise for Mr. and Mrs. Samson Sr.—we've replaced their regular honey with Lion-Grown Bee Swarm Honey."*

Now go and smite Amalek, and utterly destroy all that they have, and **spare them not**, but slay both man and woman, infant and suckling, ox and sheep, camel and ass.

1 Samuel 15:3 📖 *Don't forget to kill their puppies and kittens!*

And a certain man of the sons of the prophets said unto his neighbor in the word of the Lord, "**Smite me**, I pray thee." And the man refused to smite him. Then said he unto him, "Because thou hast not obeyed the voice of the Lord, behold, as soon as thou art departed from me, a lion shall slay thee." And as soon as he was departed from him, a lion found him and slew him.

1 Kings 20:36 ⚰ When you go around killing as many people as Jehovah, you have to mix it up occasionally. Lions, bears, snakes, and avenging angels are all valued members of his divine hit squad.

And King Solomon and all the congregation of Israel, that were assembled unto him, were before the ark, sacrificing sheep and oxen, that **could not be counted** nor numbered for multitude.

2 Chronicles 5:6 ⚰ Too many to count must mean more than 142,000 animals. See below.

And King Solomon offered a sacrifice of twenty and two thousand oxen, and a **hundred and twenty thousand sheep**. So the king and all the people dedicated the house of God.

2 Chronicles 7:5 ⚰ What god wouldn't be impressed with the deaths of 120,000 sheep?

GOING FOR A SLAY RIDE Leviticus 1-10
For being the best-selling book of all time, the Bible does contain chapters that are definitely not page turners. Try reading Leviticus 1-10 at your children's next Sunday school lesson, unless they're the kind of kids who don't like hearing about ritualized animal slaughter.

THE MOST BORING STORY EVER TOLD

Because the fate of the sons of men and the fate of the beasts is the same. As is the death of one, so is the death of the other, and all have one spirit. **Man is not higher than the beasts**, because all is to no purpose.

Ecclesiastes 3:19 ⚰ This "all one spirit" stuff may sound nice—for vegetarians, but meat lovers prefer their original "dominion over them" status.

The beasts of the field shall honor me, the jackals and the ostriches, because I give waters in the wilderness and rivers in the desert, to give drink to my people, my chosen.

Isaiah 43:20 ⚰ Which begs the question: how can you tell when a jackal is honoring you?

He who kills an ox is as he who kills a man. He who sacrifices a lamb, as he who breaks a dog's neck. He who offers an offering, as he who offers pig's blood. He who burns frankincense, as he who blesses an idol. Yes, they have chosen their own ways, and their soul delights in their abominations.

Isaiah 66:3 🖳 *Do you mean that everything I learned about how wonderful animal sacrifice is (Leviticus 1-10) turns out not to be true?*

But, so that we may not be a cause of trouble to them, go to the sea, and let down a hook, and take ***the first fish which comes up***, and in his mouth you will see a bit of money. Take that, and with it pay the tax for me and you.

Matthew 17:27 🖳 *No wonder Jesus didn't mind tax collectors. He had a secret supply of money fish, and his friends were all fishermen.*

For every kind of animal, bird, creeping thing, and thing in the sea, is tamed, and ***has been tamed by mankind***.

James 3:7 🖳 *Unfortunately, some animals have forgotten some of their training since this was written.*

PITY THE TRANSLATOR 3

Languages work in mysterious ways. You would think translating the name of an animal wouldn't be that tricky, but evidently, you've never translated the Bible before. Below is the World English Bible translation followed by various others.

❝ Will the ***wild ox*** be content to serve you? Or will he stay by your feeding trough?
Job 39:9

Shall the ***rhinoceros*** be willing to serve thee?
Douay-Rheims

Will the ***unicorn*** be willing to serve thee?
King James Version

Is a ***reem*** willing to serve thee?
Young's Literal Translation

Will the ***buffalo*** be willing to serve thee?
Darby Translation

Will the ***ox of the mountains*** be your servant?
Bible in Basic English

SLAVERY

Do you want a good justification for having a slave? The Bible is the book for you. From start to finish, the Bible sees slavery as a fact of life. The hot topic of the day wasn't whether we should abolish slavery, but rather, how hard can we beat our slaves? Of all the terrible things that are an abomination unto the Lord, slavery is not among them.

The angel of the Lord said, "Hagar, Sarai's servant, where have you come from and where are you going?" And she said, "I am running away from Sarai, my master's wife." And the angel said to her, "Go back and **put yourself under her authority**."
Genesis 16:8-9 ⚜ *An angel advises a slave to not seek her freedom! Maybe that's because angels have never known what it's like to not be under someone's authority.*

Now these are the judgments which thou shalt set before them. **If thou shalt buy a Hebrew servant**, six years he shall serve, and in the seventh he shall depart free for nothing. If he came in by himself, he shall depart by himself. If he was married, then his wife shall depart with him. If his master hath given him a wife, and she hath borne him sons or daughters, the wife and her children shall be her master's, and he shall depart by himself.
Exodus 21:1-4 ⚜ *Which do you never want to see again: your freedom or your wife and kids?*

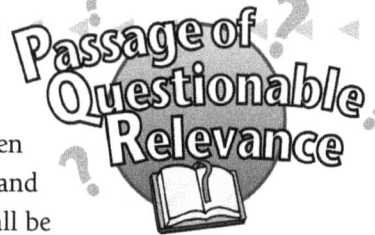

Passage of Questionable Relevance

And **if a man shall sell his daughter** to be a maid-servant, she shall not depart as the men-servants do. If she shall not please her master, who hath betrothed her to himself, then shall he let her be redeemed. To sell her to a strange nation he shall have no power, seeing he hath dealt deceitfully with her. And if he hath betrothed her to his son, he shall deal with her after the manner of daughters. If he shall take him another wife, her food, her raiment, and her duty of marriage shall he not diminish.
Exodus 21:7-11 ⚜ *Maybe it's a mistranslation and originally said, "Never sell your daughter. Ever!"*

If a man strikes his servant or his maid with a rod, and he dies under his hand, he shall surely be punished. Notwithstanding, if he gets up after a day or two, he shall not be punished, for **he is his property**.
Exodus 21:20-21 ⚜ *Translation: Be sure to perfect your slave-beating skills, so that all beaten slaves can get up within a day or so.*

If a man strikes his servant's eye or his maid's eye, and destroys it, he shall let him go free for his eye's sake. If he strikes out his man-servant's tooth or his maid-servant's tooth, he shall **let him go free for his tooth's sake**.

Exodus 21:26-27 "Note to self: knock out one of my teeth, and then the next time the master beats me, pretend it just got knocked out."

EXODUS 21:27

Don't Punch Slaves!!

UNLIKELY SIGN

From a Fan in the Stands

UNSAFE PASSAGE

Unsuitable for Student-Led Prayer

But **you may get servants as property** from among the nations round about. From them you may take men-servants and women-servants. And in addition, you may get, for money, servants from among the children of other nations who are living with you and from their families which have come to birth in your land, and these will be your property. And they will be your children's heritage after you, to keep as their property. They will be your servants forever, but you may not be hard masters to your countrymen, the children of Israel.

Leviticus 25:44-46 These biblical rules on slavery are sadly inapplicable to my 21st century lifestyle.

And it shall be, if he say unto thee, "I will not go out from thee," because he loveth thee and thy house, because he is well with thee, then **take a sharp-pointed instrument**, driving it through his ear into the door, and he will be your servant forever. And you may do the same for your servant-girl.

Deuteronomy 15:16-17 What else can you do when your servant just won't leave the house?

BIBLE FUNMENTIONABLE QUIZ

KNOW YOUR RIGHTS AS A SLAVE OWNER

According to the Bible, which are the slaver owner's DOs and which are the DON'Ts in the list below?

1 Drill a hole in the ear of a slave that won't leave you. –*Exod. 21:6*

2 Beat your slave toothless. –*Exod. 21:27*

3 Buy foreign slaves. –*Lev. 25:44*

4 Beat a slave until they are incapacitated for a day or two only. –*Exod. 21:21*

5 Pass slaves on to your children. –*Lev. 25:46*

6 Beat your slave blind. –*Exod. 21:26*

7 Make a slave of thieves who can't pay restitution. –*Exod. 22:3*

8 Expect your slave to be respectful of you, because a disrespectful slave might make all Christian teaching look bad. –*1 Tim. 6:1*

9 Beat your slave to death. –*Exod. 21:20*

10 Buy local slaves, if they are immigrants. –*Lev. 25:45*

DOs: 1,3,4,5,7,8,10   DON'Ts: 2,6,9

And the anger of the Lord was hot against Israel, and **he sold them** into the hands of the Philistines, and into the hands of the children of Ammon.

Judges 10:7 And God also sold them to nearby enemies (Judges 2:14), and again to King Chushanrishathaim of Mesopotamia (Judges 3:8), and yet again to King Jabin of Canaan (Judges 4:2). Isn't this the same God who repeatedly feels compelled to remind the Israelites that he "brought you forth out of the land of Egypt"?

Servants, do what is ordered by those who are **your natural masters**, having respect and fear for them with all your heart, as to Christ—not only under your master's eye, as pleasers of men, but as servants of Christ, doing the pleasure of God from the heart, doing your work readily, as to the Lord, and not to men, in the knowledge that for every good thing anyone does, he will have his reward from the Lord, if he is a servant or if he is free.
Ephesians 6:5-8 Slaves need pep talks too.

Servants, be subject with all fear to your masters, not only to the good and gentle, but also to the ill-tempered.

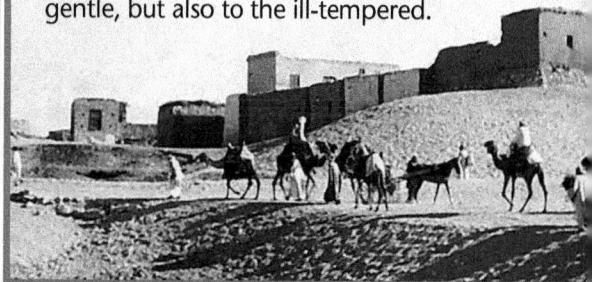

1 Peter 2:18   *Bible Funmentionables Poster Series*

Servants, **obey in all things your masters** according to the flesh; not with eye-service, as men-pleasers, but in singleness of heart, fearing God.
Colossians 3:22 Obey your masters, not because the master's watching, but because God's watching.

IF THOU KNOWETH WHAT'S GOOD FOR THEE

 Moses brought down some pretty famous "Thou shalts" from the mountain, but the Bible contains many lesser known orders from on high (or otherwise).

Thou shalt . . .
bruise his head –*Gen. 3:15*
break his neck –*Exod. 13:13*
make loops of blue –*Exod. 26:4*
make curtains of goat hair –*Exod. 26:7*
rear up the tabernacle –*Exod. 26:30*
make his pans –*Exod. 27:3*
put it under the compass –*Exod. 27:5*
fasten in the two ouches –*Exod. 28:25*
make them linen breeches –*Exod. 28:42*
gird them with girdles –*Exod. 29:9*
cut the ram in pieces –*Exod. 29:17*
sanctify the breast –*Exod. 29:27*
see my back parts –*Exod. 33:23*
bring the meat –*Lev. 2:8*
sell me meat for money –*Deu. 2:28*
surely kill him –*Deu. 13:9*
take an awl and thrust it –*Deu. 15:17*

save alive nothing –*Deu. 20:16*
have a paddle –*Deu. 23:13*
cut off her hand –*Deu. 25:12*
plaster them with plaster –*Deu. 27:4*
grope at noonday –*Deu. 28:29*
be the tail –*Deu. 28:44*
serve other gods –*Deu. 28:64*
sleep with thy fathers –*Deu. 31:16*
hough their horses –*Josh. 11:6*
have wars –*2 Chr. 16:9*
be in league with the stones –*Job 5:23*
have plenty of silver –*Job 22:25*
tread upon the lion –*Ps. 91:13*
have goats' milk –*Prov. 27:27*
also suck the milk –*Isa. 60:16*
read them in the ears –*Jer. 36:6*
be drunken –*Lam. 4:21*
be dumb –*Ezek. 3:26*

bake it with dung –*Ezek. 4:12*
be for booties –*Hab. 2:7*
heap coals of fire on his head –*Rom. 12:20*
take the ashes of perfume –*Tob. 6:16*

Thou shalt **not** . . .
revile the gods –*Exod. 22:28*
seethe a kid –*Exod. 34:26*
go up and down –*Lev. 19:16*
see thy brother's ass –*Deu. 22:4*
muzzle the ox –*Deu. 25:4*
play the harlot –*Hos. 3:3*

CIRCUMCISION

At the time the Bible was written, the possibilities for a hygienic lifestyle weren't what they are today, so circumcision may have made more sense back then. Christian theologians say that the faithful can choose to mark their son's covenant with God in the remarkably less painful procedure of baptizing them with water. Or you can always do what Abraham did and wait until he is 99 years old, to give him a chance to think it through and decide for himself.

THE UNTOLD STORY
The Deleted Details from Popular Passages

Abraham was **ninety-nine years old** when he underwent circumcision.
Genesis 17:24 📖 A rare surgical procedure among nonagenarians.

UNSAFE PASSAGE
Unsuitable for Student-Led Prayer

The sons of Jacob answered Shechem and his father deceitfully, being enraged at the deflowering of their sister, "We cannot do what you demand, nor give our sister to one that is uncircumcised, which with us is unlawful and abominable. But in this way may we be allied with you: if you will be like us, and all the male sex among you be circumcised, then will we mutually give and take your daughters and ours, and we will dwell with you and will be one people." And they all agreed and circumcised all the males. And on the third day, **when the pain of the wound was greatest**, two of the sons of Jacob, Simeon and Levi, the brothers of Dinah, taking their swords, entered boldly into the city and slew all the men. They killed also Hamor and Shechem, and took away their sister Dinah out of Shechem's house. And when they were gone out, the other sons of Jacob came upon the slain and plundered the city in revenge of the rape. They took their sheep and their herds and their asses, wasting all they had in their houses and in the fields, and their children and wives they took captive.
Genesis 34:13-16,24-29 📖 Ah yes, the old convince-all-the-grown-men-to-needlessly-circumcise-themselves-then-kill-them-and-take-their-livestock-women-and-children trick.

It happened on the way at a lodging place, that **Yahweh met Moses and wanted to kill him**. Then Zipporah took a flint, and cut off the foreskin of her son, and cast it at his feet, and she said, "Surely a bloody husband are you to me."
Exodus 4:24-25 📖 Moses, God's about to kill you! Quick, somebody throw a foreskin!

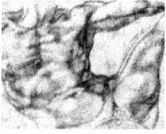

At that time the Lord said unto Joshua, "Make thee sharp knives, and **circumcise again the children** of Israel the second time."

Joshua 5:2 ☙ Which makes you wonder just how many times a guy can get circumcised.

And Saul said, "Thus shall ye say to David, 'The king desireth not any dowry, but **a hundred foreskins of the Philistines**, to be avenged of the king's enemies.'" Now Saul thought to make David fall by the hand of the Philistines. And David arose and went, he and his men, and slew of the Philistines two hundred men. And David brought their foreskins, and they gave them in full number to the king, that he might be the king's son-in-law. And Saul gave him Michal his daughter to wife.

1 Samuel 18:25,27 ☙ "Great, now what am I going to do with these 100 extra foreskins?"

They, when they heard it, glorified God. They said to him, "You see, brother, how many thousands there are among the Jews of those who have believed, and they are all zealous for the law. They have been informed about you, that you teach all the Jews who are among the Gentiles to forsake Moses, telling them **not to circumcise their children**, neither to walk after the customs."

Acts 21:20-21 ☙ Just in case you thought he was just talking about boys, Paul is clearly referring to both genders here.

For circumcision indeed profits, if you are a doer of the law, but if you are a transgressor of the law, your **circumcision has become uncircumcision**.

Romans 2:25 ☙ This is a good way to check to see if you're a doer or a transgressor.

Circumcision is nothing, and its opposite is nothing, but only doing the orders of God is of value.

1 Corinthians 7:19 ☙ That's how you stake out a neutral position. Just don't tell Abraham that circumcision is nothing.

See, I Paul say to you, that if you undergo circumcision, **Christ will be of no use to you**.

Galatians 5:2 ☙ Forget that he's talking about circumcision—you just don't expect a lot of Bible passages about Christ being of no use.

Jesus' disciples said unto him, "Is circumcision beneficial or is it not?" He said to them, "If it were beneficial, children's fathers would produce them **circumcised already from their mothers**."

Gospel of Thomas #53 ☙ And the same goes for tongue piercing. If God really wanted you to have one of those, you would have been born that way.

HAIR

The writers of the Bible took their hair care surprisingly seriously, and some believers actually turn to the Bible for advice on biblically sanctioned hair styles. Wouldn't we all be better off if the Bible had clearly stated, "Ye shall not take grooming advice from a 3,000-year-old book, rather findst thou a competent beautician."

The man whose hair falleth off from his head, he is **bald and clean**. And if the hair fall from his forehead, he is bald before and clean.

Leviticus 13:40-41 ※ Bald is beautiful . . . and clean too!

Ye shall not shave the **corners of your head round**, neither shalt thou mutilate the corners of thy beard.

Leviticus 19:27 ※ The first precept is easy: no bowl cuts. But on the second one, I don't know if I could find a corner of a beard and mutilate it if I tried.

So Hanun took David's servants, and after shaving off **half of their beards**, and cutting off their garments in the middle, even to their buttocks, he sent them away. When they told it unto David, he sent to meet them, because the men were greatly ashamed. And the king said, "Stay at Jericho until your beards be grown, and then return."

2 Samuel 10:4-5 ※ Or maybe shave the half beard, patch your pants, and get back to work.

And when Absalom had his hair cut, which he did at the end of every year, because it was heavy on him, the weight of **the hair was five pounds** by the king's weight.

2 Samuel 14:26 ※ Absalom never heard of going in for a trim? At times the Bible has been suspected of exaggerating in order to impress, but keep in mind that some people wet their hair before cutting it. Plus, who knows what kind of wildlife might have found a home in Absalom's mane over the course of a year.

In those days also saw I Jews that had married wives of Ashdod, of Ammon, and of Moab. And their children spake half in the speech of Ashdod, and could not speak in the Jews' language, but according to the language of each people. And I contended with them, and cursed them, and smote certain of them, and **plucked off their hair**, and made them swear by God, saying, "Ye shall not give your daughters unto their sons, nor take their daughters unto your sons or for yourselves."

Nehemiah 13:23-2 ※ "I'll teach you to not have a mixed marriage. Would you prefer a hair-plucking or a good old-fashioned smiting?"

TOP TEN
The Best of the Worst

He went up from there to Bethel, and as he was going up by the way, there came forth young lads out of the city, and mocked him, and said to him, "Go up, you baldy. Go up, you baldhead." He looked behind him, and saw them, and cursed them in the name of Yahweh. There came forth two she-bears out of the wood and mauled forty-two lads of them.

2 Kings 2:23-24 🖾 *God says don't call the bald bald. They know they're bald—and may kill you with bears.*

Baldness is come upon Gaza. Ashkelon is brought to nought, the remnant of their valley. How long wilt thou cut thyself?

Jeremiah 47:5 🖾 *Current theological thought is that baldness is actually a blessing, considering the cost savings from shampoo and hair spray alone.*

Doesn't even nature itself teach you that **if a man has long hair, it is a dishonor to him**? But if a woman has long hair, it is a glory to her, for her hair is given to her for a covering.

1 Corinthians 11:14-15 🖾 *Are you a shaved and shorn again Christian?*

Do not let your ornaments be those of the body such as **dressing of the hair** or putting on of jewels of gold or fair clothing.

1 Peter 3:3 🖾 *This is the biblically sanctioned rebuttal for when your parents won't let you wear your favorite tattered jeans to church.*

FOOD

Eve famously ate the unidentified fruit from the tree of the knowledge of good and evil. If she hadn't done that, we could all still be luxuriating in Eden, as happy as chimps or some other lower primate with even less self-awareness. Fortunately, the Bible gives all of us fallen folks the knowledge of the good and evil foods, though oddly no warning about the dangers of eating blowfish and hawksbill turtles. Bon appétit!

And Esau saith unto Jacob, "Let me eat, I pray thee, **some of this red red thing**, for I am weary." Therefore was his name called Edom.
Genesis 25:30 📖 *Conversely, if you're overly excited, try eating a blue blue thing.*

And Aaron shall lay both his hands upon the head of the live goat and confess over him all the iniquities of the children of Israel and all their transgressions in all their sins, putting them **upon the head of the goat**, and shall send him away by the hand of a fit man into the wilderness.
Exodus 16:21 📖 *Was food so abundant that they could send off the "scapegoat" whenever they sinned?*

The first of the first-fruits of thy ground thou shalt bring unto the house of Jehovah thy God. Thou shalt not **boil a kid in its mother's milk**.
Exodus 34:26 📖 *Keep this in mind the next time you use your* Cooking with Kids *cookbook.*

And these ye shall have in abomination **among the birds. They shall not be eaten**. They are an abomination: the eagle, and the gier-eagle, and the osprey, and the kite, and the falcon after its kind, every raven after its kind, and the ostrich, and the night-hawk, and the seamew, and the hawk after its kind, and the little owl, and the cormorant, and the great owl, and the horned owl, and the pelican, and the vulture, and the stork, the heron after its kind, and the hoopoe, and **the bat**.
Leviticus 11:13-19 📖 *I'm not saying, "Go eat a bat," but as the bat is a mammal, it might not belong on a list of inedible birds.*

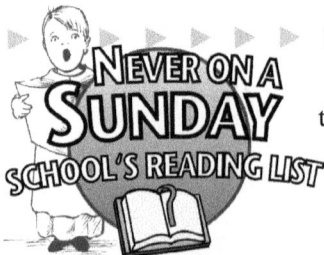

Even these of them **ye may eat: the locust** after its kind, and the bald locust after its kind, and the cricket after its kind, and the grasshopper after its kind. But all winged creeping things, which have four feet, are an abomination unto you.
Leviticus 11:22-23 📖 *We all know that insects have six legs, unless you were to manually remove two of them—in which case, don't eat them.*

NEVER ON A SUNDAY SCHOOL'S READING LIST

Say you to the people, "Sanctify yourselves against tomorrow, and you shall eat flesh. For you have wept in the ears of Yahweh, saying, 'Who shall give us flesh to eat? for it was well with us in Egypt.' Therefore, Yahweh will give you flesh, and you shall eat. You shall not eat one day, nor two days, nor five days, neither ten days, nor twenty days, but a whole month, **until it come out at your nostrils**, and it be loathsome to you; because you have rejected Yahweh who is among you and have wept before him, saying, 'Why came we forth out of Egypt?'"

Numbers 11:18-20 ⚔ So to recap this really cool trick, weep in God's ear, and meat will come out of your nose.

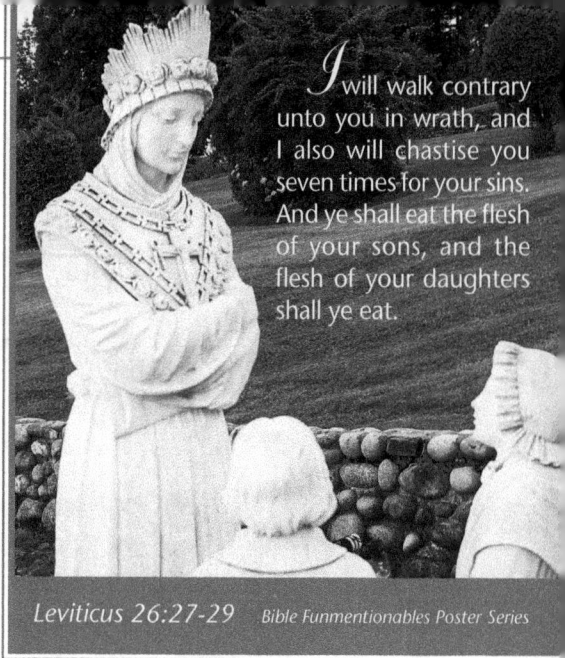

I will walk contrary unto you in wrath, and I also will chastise you seven times for your sins. And ye shall eat the flesh of your sons, and the flesh of your daughters shall ye eat.

Leviticus 26:27-29   Bible Funmentionables Poster Series

And it came to pass, that on the morrow Moses went into the tabernacle of witness, and behold, the rod of Aaron for the house of Levi was budded, and brought forth buds, and bloomed blossoms, and **yielded almonds**.

Numbers 17:8 ⚔ And the next day the almonds were available in honey-roasted and ranch flavors.

UNSAFE PASSAGE
Unsuitable for Student-Led Prayer

When thou comest into thy neighbor's vineyard, **then thou mayest eat of grapes thy fill** at thine own pleasure. But thou shalt not put any in thy vessel. When thou comest into thy neighbor's standing grain, then thou mayest pluck the ears with thy hand, but thou shalt not move a sickle unto thy neighbor's standing grain.

Deuteronomy 23:24-25 ⚔ Remember to write a nice thank you note afterwards.

And the angel said to them, "Peace be to you; fear not. For when I was with you, I was there by the will of God. Bless ye him, and sing praises to him. I seemed indeed to eat and to drink with you, but I used an **invisible meat and drink** which cannot be seen by men."

Tobit 12:17-19 ⚔ Though nutritionally it's not at all unhealthful to consume invisible food, it is difficult to mass market.

EDIBLE OR INEDIBLE?
The Bible's Divine Dining Guide

DO EAT:	DON'T EAT:		
arbeh	baby goat (boiled in its mom's milk)	crocodile	lapwing	rock badger
attacus		cuckoo	larus	sea eagle
beetle	bat	eagle	lizards (various)	seafood (without fins and scales)
bruchus	bittern	falcon	mole	
cricket	camel	ferret	mouse	
grasshopper	chadrion	gecko	osprey	seamew
hargab	chameleon	gier-eagle	ossifrage	skink
hargol	cherogrillus	griffon	ostrich	snail
katydid	chomet	gull	owls (various)	stellio
locust	coney	hare	pelican	stork
ophiomachus	cormorant	hawk	pig	swan
solam	creeping animals (except those mentioned under "Do Eat")	heron	porphyrion	tortoise
your neighbor's produce (one handful limit)		hoopoe	rabbit	vulture
	ibis	rat	weasel
	kite	raven	

Thou hast broken the heads of the dragon. Thou hast **given him to be meat** for the people of the Ethiopians.

Psalms 74:14 📖 *Eating dragon head meat is either a terrible curse or possibly a foreign delicacy.*

He that withholds corn, the people shall curse him, but blessing shall be on the head of him that sells it.

Proverbs 11:26 📖 *Blessed are those people that sell corn in those little roadside shacks.*

A word fitly spoken is like **apples of gold** in baskets of silver.

Proverbs 25:11 📖 *Would apples made out of gold be really tasty, or do you just sell them for the gold in them?*

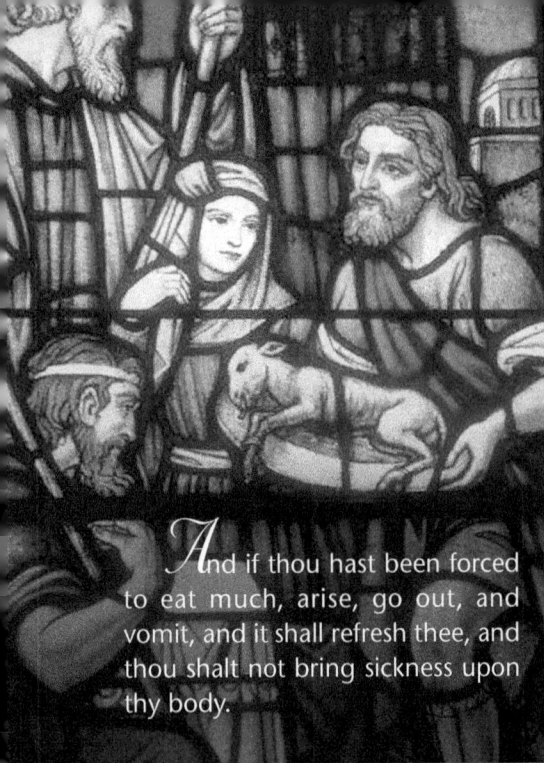

And if thou hast been forced to eat much, arise, go out, and vomit, and it shall refresh thee, and thou shalt not bring sickness upon thy body.

Sirach 31:25   Bible Funmentionables Poster Series

Have you found honey? Eat as much as is sufficient for you, lest you **eat too much and vomit it**.

Proverbs 25:16 📖 *Have I found honey? Well, no, not recently.*

And it will be in that day that a man will give food to a young cow and two sheep, and they will give so much milk that he will be able to have **butter for his food**, for butter and honey will be the food of all who are still living in the land.

Isaiah 7:21-22 📖 *Butter and honey: part of a complete breakfast!*

And one shall snatch on the right hand and be hungry, and he shall eat on the left hand and shall not be satisfied. **They shall eat every man the flesh of his own arm**.

Isaiah 9:20 📖 *Eating your own flesh: an harmless activity.*

For with fire and sword will the Lord come, judging all the earth, and his sword will be on all flesh. And great numbers will be put to death by him. As for those who keep themselves separate, and make themselves clean in the gardens, going after one in the middle, taking pig's flesh for food, and other **disgusting things, such as the mouse**: their works and their thoughts will come to an end together, says the Lord.

Isaiah 66:16-17 📖 *God will smite all clean, garden-dwelling mice-eaters—which is fortunately a small percentage of society.*

TOP TEN
The Best of the Worst

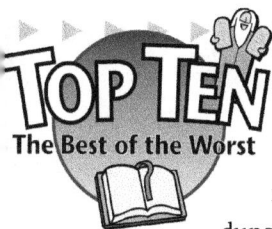

And thou shalt eat it as barley cakes, and thou shalt **bake it with human excrement** in their sight. Then he said to me, "Lo, I have given thee cow's dung for man's dung, and thou shalt prepare thy bread with them."

Ezekiel 4:12,15 "I don't care if you say you use a secret ingredient in your bread. You know what I think it tastes like?"

One of their prophets has said, "The men of Crete are ever false, evil beasts, **lovers of food**, hating work."

Titus 1:12 No better way to enshrine a stereotype than by putting it in your most sacred book.

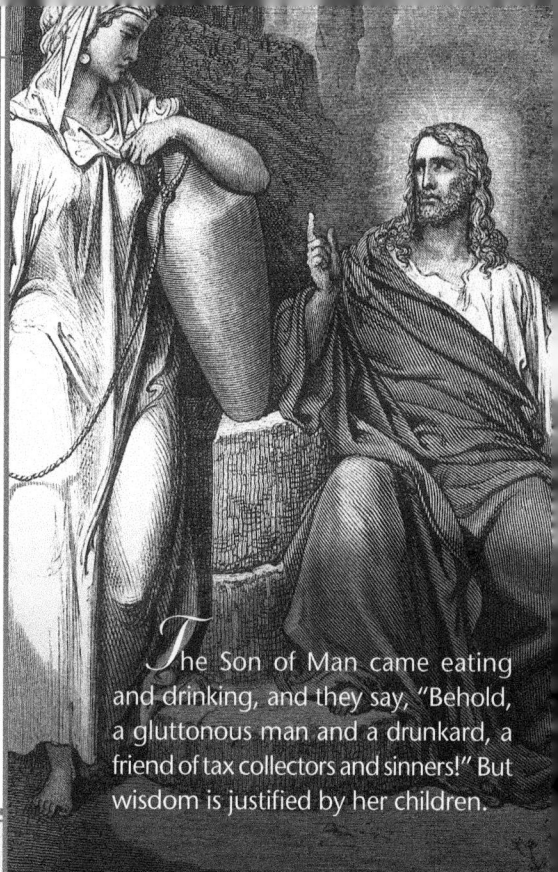

The Son of Man came eating and drinking, and they say, "Behold, a gluttonous man and a drunkard, a friend of tax collectors and sinners!" But wisdom is justified by her children.

Matthew 11:19 — Bible Funmentionables Poster Series

BIBLE FUNMENTIONABLES QUIZ
YOU CAN'T KEEP A GOOD BOOK DOWN

Have you been exposed to a wide range of Bible passages, or were you only taught the nice and safe ones? See if you are able to fill in the blanks below with the correct biblical term.

And with which the land is defiled: the abominations of which I will visit, that it may _____ out its inhabitants. *Leviticus 18:25*

Beware then, lest in like manner, it _____ you also out, if you do the like things, as it _____ed out the nation that was before you. *Leviticus 18:28*

The riches which he hath swallowed, he shall _____ up. *Job 20:15*

The meats which thou hadst eaten, thou shalt _____ up. *Proverbs 23:8*

As a dog that returneth to his _____, so is the fool that repeateth his folly. *Proverbs 26:11*

The Lord hath mingled in the midst thereof the spirit of giddiness, and they have caused Egypt to err in all its works, as drunken men stagger and _____. *Isaiah 19:14*

For all tables were full of _____ and filth. *Isaiah 28:8*

And thou shalt say to them, "Thus saith the Lord of hosts the God of Israel: 'Drink ye, and be drunken, and _____.'" *Jeremiah 25:27*

And the Lord spoke to the fish, and it _____ed out Jonah upon the dry land. *Jonah 2:10*

Answer: Did you throw up your hands and spew invectives trying to answer this? If the question ever comes up again, you'll know the answer is "vomit."

DRINK

Some people feel bad about drinking because the Bible disapproves of it. Some people feel bad about not drinking because the Bible approves of it. It's confusing enough to make you start drinking, or quit drinking, as the case may be.

He took the calf which they had made, and burnt it with fire, ground it to powder, scattered it on the water, and **made the children of Israel drink of it**.
Exodus 32:20 ⚒ Make mine de-calf.

Moreover, also a famine hath come upon them, and for drought of water they are already to be counted among the dead. And they have a design even to kill their cattle and to **drink the blood** of them.
Judith 11:10-11 ⚒ "Hmm…die of thirst or drink cow's blood. I'm thinking. I'm thinking."

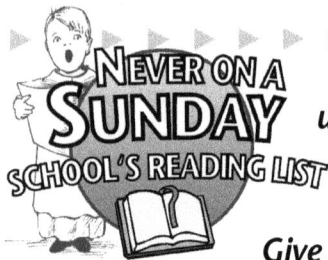

NEVER ON A SUNDAY SCHOOL'S READING LIST

If thy enemy be hungry, give him to eat. If he thirst, give him water to drink. For thou shalt **heap hot coals upon his head**, and the Lord will reward thee.
Proverbs 25:21-22 ⚒ I think I saw this in a Three Stooges episode.

Give strong drink unto him that is ready to perish, and wine unto the bitter of soul. Let him drink, and forget his poverty, and remember his misery no more.
Proverbs 31:6-7 ⚒ Some people could really use a drink, sayeth the Lord.

THE BIBLE ON IMBIBING

⚒ Looking for clear moral guidance? Decide whether drinking alcohol is right for you based on the passages below.

PRO
Deuteronomy 7:13 – Having wine is a sign of God's blessing.
Sirach 31:36 – Wine in moderation brings joy.
Matthew 11:19 – Jesus had a reputation for drinking.
1 Timothy 5:23 – Wine is good for the stomach.

CON
Proverbs 20:1 – Drinking is unwise.
Proverbs 21:17 – Loving wine makes you poor.
Isaiah 5:11 – Drinking all day is cursed.
Titus 2:3 – Old women shouldn't drink too much.

Wine was created from the beginning to make men joyful, and not to make them drunk. Wine drunken with moderation is the joy of the soul and the heart. **Sober drinking** is health to soul and body.
Ecclesiastes 31:35-37 ⚒ The Bible, in being able to distinguish between use and abuse, provides accurate medical advice way ahead of its time.

And nd they have cast lots upon my people, and the boy they have put in the stews, and the girl they have sold for wine, that they might drink.

Joel 3:3

Bible Funmentionables Poster Series

Let my beloved come into his garden, and eat the fruit of his apple trees. I am come into my garden, O my sister, my spouse, I have gathered my myrrh, with my aromatical spices. I have eaten the honeycomb with my honey, **I have drunk my wine with my milk**. Eat, O friends, and drink, and be inebriated, my dearly beloved.

Song of Songs 5:1 🍷 *Does this guy know how to party or what?*

Woe to him that giveth drink to his friend, and presenteth his gall, and maketh him drunk, that he may behold his nakedness. Thou art filled with shame instead of glory. Drink thou also, and fall fast asleep. The cup of the right hand of the Lord shall compass thee, and shameful vomiting shall be on thy glory.

Habakkuk 2:15-16 🍷 *And then it's so hard to get your glory really clean again after that.*

But I say unto you, I will not drink henceforth of this fruit of the vine, until that day when I drink it new with you **in my Father's kingdom**.

Matthew 26:29 🍷 *Another reason to aim for heaven: to party with Jesus!*

Do not take only water as your drink, but **take a little wine** for the good of your stomach and because you are frequently ill.

1 Timothy 5:23 🍷 *Thanks, Dr. Paul!*

SPECIAL EFFECTS

People have always thrilled to stories of action and excitement, with factual accuracy being a lesser concern. The Bible delivers imaginative, over-the-top visuals like raining fire, ceaseless bloodshed, and ferocious dragons, without which it would be just a boring ol' book of proverbs (no offense, Book of Proverbs). And . . . action!

Then Moses and Aaron went in to Pharaoh, and they did as the Lord had said. And Aaron put his rod down on the earth before Pharaoh and his servants, and it became a snake. Then Pharaoh sent for the wise men and the wonder-workers, and they, the wonder-workers of Egypt, did the same with their secret arts. For every one of them put down his rod on the earth, and **they became snakes**, but Aaron's rod made a meal of their rods.

> Exodus 7:10-12 *Here's a lesson for today's magicians who have their tricks stolen by lesser talents: have the animal in your trick eat your competitor's animal. The crowd loves it when you go the extra mile like that.*

And they came across Adoni-zedek, and made war on him, and they overcame the Canaanites and the Perizzites. But Adoni-zedek went in flight, and they went after him, and overtook him, and had **his thumbs and his great toes cut off**.

> Judges 1:5-6 *"Oh great, now how is he going to sign the terms of surrender?"*

So Samson went and got three hundred foxes and some sticks of fire-wood, and **he put the foxes tail-to-tail** with a stick between every two tails. Then firing the sticks, he let the foxes loose among the uncut grain of the Philistines, and all the corded stems as well as the living grain and the vine-gardens and the olives went up in flames.

> Judges 15:4-5 *Capturing 300 foxes: Not easy. Putting foxes tail-to-tail: Really not easy. Burning down all of the fields and vineyards of your enemy: Priceless.*

And that night **the angel of the Lord** went out and put to death in the army of the As-syrians a hundred and eighty-five thousand men, and when the people got up early in the morning, there was nothing to be seen but dead bodies.

> 2 Kings 19:35 *A mortician's dream.*

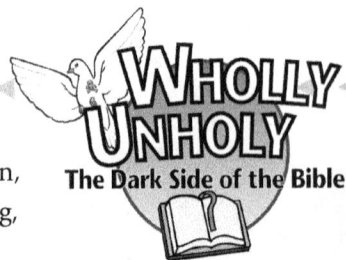

WHOLLY UNHOLY
The Dark Side of the Bible

And again there was war at Gath, where there was a very tall man who had **twenty-four fingers and toes**, six fingers on his hands and six toes on his feet. He also was the son of the giant.

2 Samuel 21:20 and 1 Chronicles 20:6 🕮 *"Hey, let's cut off this guy's thumbs and big toes!" (See Judges 1:5-6 on the facing page.) — "No, that's just what he'd want us to do."*

The sword of the Lord is filled with blood. It is made thick with the blood of lambs and buck goats, with the blood of rams full of marrow. For there is a victim of the Lord in Bosra and a great slaughter in the land of Edom. And the unicorns shall go down with them, and the bulls with the mighty. Their land shall be soaked with blood, and their ground with the fat of fat ones.

Isaiah 34:6-7 🕮 *You try rubbing, you try scrubbing, but you still get thick lamb and goat blood on your sword.*

And the angel of the Lord went out and put to death in the army of the Assyrians a hundred and eighty-five thousand men, and when the people got up early in the morning, there was **nothing to be seen but dead bodies**.

Isaiah 37:36 🕮 *When the same passage appears in the Bible twice, it must be true. (See 2 Kings 19:35 on the facing page.)*

Behold, I will cause the shadow on the sundial, which has gone down on the sundial of Ahaz with the sun, to return backward ten steps. So **the sun returned ten steps on the sundial** on which it had gone down.

Isaiah 38:7-8 🕮 *The earth reversed its rotation and switched back again. Who hasn't prayed for this miracle when they're running a little late?*

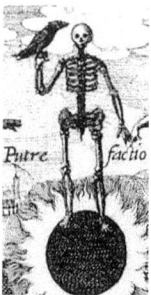

And again he said to me, "**Be a prophet to these bones**, and say to them, 'O you dry bones, give ear to the word of the Lord. This is what the Lord has said to these bones, "See, I will make breath come into you so that you may come to life."'" So I gave the word as I was ordered, and at my words there was a shaking of the earth, and the bones came together, bone to bone. And looking I saw that there were muscles on them and flesh came up, and they were covered with skin, but there was no breath in them. And I gave the word at his orders, and breath came into them, and they came to life and got up on their feet, a very great army.

Ezekiel 37:4,5,7,8,10 🕮 *Just because you <u>can</u> create an army of skeleton people, doesn't mean you <u>should</u>. Just remember to use your superpowers for good and not for evil.*

Then Daniel took pitch, and fat, and hair, and boiled them together, and he made lumps and put them into the dragon's mouth, and **the dragon burst asunder**. And he said, "Behold him whom you worshipped."

Daniel 14:26 🕮 *Let that be a lesson to all those dragon worshippers out there.*

It came to pass also, that seven brethren, together with their mother, were apprehended and compelled by the king to eat swine's flesh against the law, for which end they were tormented with whips and scourges. But one of them, who was the eldest, said thus, "What wouldst thou ask or learn from us? We are ready to die rather than to transgress the laws of God, received from our fathers." Then the king being angry commanded frying pans, and brazen caldrons to be made hot, which forthwith being heated, he commanded to cut out the tongue of him that had spoken first, and the skin of his head being drawn off, to chop off also the extremities of his hands and feet, the rest of his brethren, and his mother, looking on. And when he was now maimed in all parts, he commanded him, being yet alive, to be brought to the fire, and to be **fried in the frying pan**. And while he was suffering therein long torments, the rest, together with the mother, exhorted one another to die manfully.

2 Maccabees 7:1-5 🕮 *"Fry like a man."*

THE UNTOLD STORY
The Deleted Details from Popular Passages

Jesus cried again with a loud voice, and yielded up his spirit. Behold, the veil of the temple was torn in two from the top to the bottom. The earth quaked and the rocks were split. The tombs were opened, and **many bodies of the saints** who had fallen asleep were raised. And coming forth out of the tombs after his resurrection, they entered into the holy city and appeared to many.

Matthew 27:50-53 🕮 The Greatest Story Ever Told *meets* Night of the Living Dead.

And upon a day appointed, Herod being arrayed in kingly apparel, sat in the judgment seat and made an oration to them. And the people made acclamation, saying, "It is the voice of a god and not of a man." And forthwith an angel of the Lord struck him, because he had not given the honor to God, and being **eaten up by worms**, he gave up the ghost.

Acts 12:21-23 🕮 *How was Herod like a church council? He was the diet of worms.*

A certain young man named Eutychus sat in the window, weighed down with deep sleep. **As Paul spoke still longer**, being weighed down by his sleep, he fell down from the third story and was taken up dead.

Acts 20:9 📖 *The experienced public speaker will see this as a pretty clear sign that it's time to wrap up.*

And I took the little book out of the angel's hand and **ate it up**, and it was in my mouth sweet as honey. And as soon as I had eaten it, my belly was bitter.

Revelation 10:10 📖 *Don't judge a book by its sweet-as-honey flavor.*

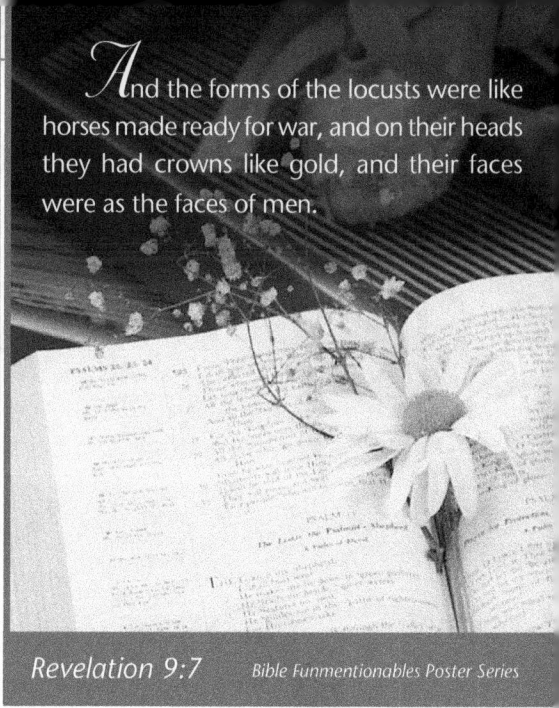

*A*nd the forms of the locusts were like horses made ready for war, and on their heads they had crowns like gold, and their faces were as the faces of men.

Revelation 9:7   *Bible Funmentionables Poster Series*

These are the two olive trees and the two candlesticks standing before the God of the earth. And if any man will hurt them, **fire proceedeth out of their mouth**, and devoureth their enemies. And if any man will hurt them, he must in this manner be killed.

Revelation 11:4-5 📖 *The symbol for peace: an olive branch. The symbol for instant, horrific death: God's weaponized, flame-throwing olive tree.*

And there appeared another wonder in heaven. And behold a great red dragon, having seven heads, and ten horns, and seven crowns upon his heads. And there was war in heaven. **Michael and his angels fought against the dragon**. The dragon and his angels fought and prevailed not.

Revelation 12:3,7 📖 *It is a relief to know that heaven has appeared to have successfully dealt with their dragon infestation. Although a dragon war from time to time might spice up the occasional monotony that comes with eternal life.*

And I saw an angel standing in the sun, and he cried with a loud voice, saying to all the birds that fly in mid-heaven, "Come and be gathered together unto the great supper of God, that ye may **eat the flesh of kings**, and the flesh of captains, and the flesh of mighty men, and the flesh of horses and of them that sit thereon, and the flesh of all men, both free and bond, and small and great."

Revelations 19:17-18 📖 *A king fit for a meal.*

I saw an angel coming down from heaven, having the **key of the bottomless pit** and a great chain in his hand. And he laid hold on the dragon, that old serpent, which is the Devil and Satan, and bound him a thousand years, and cast him into the bottomless pit, and it was shut and locked over him, that he should deceive the nations no more, till the thousand years should be fulfilled. After this he will be let loose for a little time.

Revelation 20:1-3 📖 *Unlocking and retrieving something out of a bottomless pit is a job for no mere mortal.*

MISTAKES

Be they exaggerations, mistranslations, or just horrible ideas, these are statements that strain credulity to the point of disbelief. Let's not be too critical though. As it says in Psalms 19:12, "Forgive me from hidden errors."

THE UNTOLD STORY
The Deleted Details from Popular Passages

The earth brought forth grass, herbs yielding seed after their kind, and **trees bearing fruit** with its seed in it, after their kind, and God saw that it was good. There was evening, and there was morning, a third day.

God made the two great lights: **the greater light to rule the day**, and the lesser light to rule the night. He also made the stars. There was evening, and there was morning, a fourth day.

Genesis 1:12-13,16,19 ⛰ Sun-loving plants appear one day before the sun does—mysterious ways indeed.

And the whole earth was of **one language** and of one speech.

Genesis 11:1 ⛰ Linguists have ruled out the possibility that the "one language" was Greenlandic Norse, Esperanto, or Flemish (as Flemish is not actually a language). Just 8,000 more languages to rule out.

Jacob, however, took fresh-cut branches from poplar, almond and plane trees and made white stripes on them by peeling the bark and exposing the white inner wood of the branches. Then he placed the peeled branches in all the watering troughs, so that they would be directly in front of the flocks when they came to drink. When the flocks were in heat and came to drink, **they mated in front of the branches**, and they bore young that were streaked, or speckled, or spotted.

Genesis 30:37-39 ⛰ Jacob made Laban's unspotted goats have spotted kids by having them look at striped wood when they met for drinks at the watering hole. (He got to keep the spotted kids for himself.) Voltaire extended this logic by saying that since goats often see grass while mating, their kids should be born green.

When I was gone up into the mount to receive the tables of stone, even the tables of the covenant which Jehovah made with you, then I abode in the mount **forty days and forty nights**. I did neither eat bread nor drink water.

Deuteronomy 9:9 ⛰ Ask your doctor if the Moses Diet™ is right for you. After a week without water, serious side effects may occur, including death.

Yahweh said, "Because the cry of Sodom and Gomorrah is great, and because their sin is very grievous, **I will go down now and see** whether their deeds are as bad as the reports which have come to me. If not, I will know."

Genesis 18:20-21 📖 *Good old-fashioned legwork is crucial for even the most omniscient deity.*

Behold, the virgin shall be with child and shall bring forth a son, and they shall **call his name Immanuel**, which is, being interpreted, God with us. And Joseph arose from his sleep, and did as the angel of the Lord commanded him, and took unto him his wife, and knew her not till she had brought forth a son, and **he called his name Jesus**.

Matthew 1:23-25 📖 *Weren't they supposed to name him Immanuel?*

He put another story before them, saying, "The kingdom of heaven is like a grain of mustard seed which a man took and put in his field, which is **smaller than all seeds**. But when it has come up it is greater than the plants, and becomes a tree, so that the birds of heaven come and make their resting-places in its branches."

Matthew 13:31-32 📖 *Jesus is either not omniscient or he's stretching the truth to make a point, as the mustard seed is not the smallest seed out there.*

TOP TEN
The Best of the Worst

And these signs will be with those who have faith: in my name they will send out evil spirits, and they will make use of new languages. They will take up snakes, and if there is **poison in their drink**, it will do them no evil. They will put their hands on those who are ill, and they will get well."

Mark 16:17-18 📖 *Now there's a way to prove your faith: chug a tall glass of poison.*

MARK 16:18 **Drink Poison!**
UNLIKELY SIGN
From a Fan in the Stands

📖 SCRIBES GONE WILD

Do you have trouble distinguishing one book of the Bible from the next? Follow along to see how the introductory lines of the book of Ezra got repeated to become the final lines of the previous book, 2 Chronicles.

2   *All the days of its desolation it kept sabbath, to fulfill seventy years.*

C (2 Chronicles should have ended here, but instead it copies the first two and a half verses from Ezra.)

H *And in the first year of Cyrus king of Persia, that the word of Jehovah by the mouth of Jeremiah might be accomplished, Jehovah*
R *stirred up the spirit of Cyrus king of Persia, and he made a proclamation throughout his kingdom, and also in writing, saying, "Thus*
O *says Cyrus king of Persia, 'All the kingdoms of the earth has Jehovah the God of the heavens given to me, and he has charged me*
     to build him a house at Jerusalem, which is in Judah. Whosoever there is among you of all his people, Jehovah his God be with him,
N *and let him go up.'"*

(2 Chronicles ends mid-sentence with "and let him go up." Now Ezra gets to tell the whole story.)

E *And in the first year of Cyrus king of Persia, that the word of Jehovah by the mouth of Jeremiah might be accomplished, Jehovah*
     stirred up the spirit of Cyrus king of Persia, and he made a proclamation throughout his kingdom, and also in writing, saying, "Thus
Z *says Cyrus king of Persia, 'All the kingdoms of the earth has Jehovah the God of the heavens given to me, and he has charged me*
R *to build him a house at Jerusalem, which is in Judah. Whosoever there is among you of all his people, his God be with him,*
     and let him go up to Jerusalem, which is in Judah, and build the house of Jehovah the God of Israel. He is the God who
A *is at Jerusalem.'"*

BAD ADVICE

Some advice found in the Bible is simple and sound by today's standards. The following verses are about as helpful as Noah welcoming the big predators onto the ark that he built specifically in order to protect all those cute, fuzzy, and tasty little animals.

If a bull gores a man or a woman to death, the bull shall surely be stoned, and its flesh shall not be eaten, but the owner of the bull shall not be held responsible. But if the bull had a habit of goring in the past, and it has been testified to its owner, and he has not kept it in, but it has killed a man or a woman, the bull shall be stoned, and its owner shall also be put to death.

Exodus 21:28-29 ⚰ Only you can prevent bull gorings.

And when you have come into the land, and have put in all sorts of fruit trees, their fruit will be as if they had not had circumcision. And **for three years** their fruit may not be used for food. And in the fourth year all the fruit will be holy as a praise-offering to the Lord. But in the fifth year you may take the fruit and the increase of it for your food: I am the Lord your God.

Leviticus 19:23-25 ⚰ But nobody is saying you can't make a festive, decorative hat with all that fruit.

And Moses made a **serpent of brass**, and put it upon a pole, and it came to pass, that if a serpent had bitten any man, when he beheld the serpent of brass, he was made well.

Numbers 21:9 ⚰ Snake bite antidotes are the preferred treatment for most people these days.

For the king's navy, once in three years, went with the navy of Hiram by sea to Tharsis, and brought from thence gold, and silver, and **elephants' teeth**, and apes, and peacocks.

1 Kings 10:22 ⚰ I understand the gold and silver, and apes might be fun for a while, but elephants' teeth? Was there some sort of shortage of industrial-strength paperweights?

The fool hath said in his heart, "There is no God." They are corrupt, they have done abominable works. There is **none that doeth good**.

Psalms 14:1 ⚔ Atheists' reputations have come a long way since then. Some people are now of the opinion that a few atheists may have actually done some good at one time.

Passage of Questionable Relevance

Then Tobias asked the angel, and said to him, "I beseech thee, brother Azarias, tell me **what remedies are these things good for**, which thou hast bid me keep of the fish?" And the angel, answering, said to him, "If thou put a little piece of its heart upon coals, the smoke thereof driveth away all kind of devils, either from man or from woman, so that they come no more to them. And the gall is good for anointing the eyes, in which there is a white speck, and they shall be cured."

Tobit 6:7-9 ⚔ Fish cures are nice, but would it have broken some kind of angels' code to give us some more practical medical advice such as the germ theory of disease, the benefits of penicillin, or how about a simple warning about the danger of using thalidomide during pregnancy?

For three things the earth trembles, and under four it can't bear up: for a servant when he is king, **a fool when he is filled with food**, for an unloved woman when she is married, and a handmaid who is heir to her mistress.

Proverbs 30:21-23 ⚔ The Bible's top four pet peeves.

And he went **between the feet of the elephant**, and put himself under it, and slew it, and it fell to the ground upon him, and he died there.

1 Maccabees 6:46 ⚔ "You'll be crushed to death while being covered in piping hot elephant guts. Any volunteers?"

But I say to you that whoever looketh on a woman to lust after her, hath committed adultery with her already in his heart. And if thy right eye shall cause thee to sin, pluck it out, and cast it from thee, for it is profitable for thee that one of thy members should perish, and not that thy whole body should be cast into hell. And if **thy right hand** shall cause thee to sin, cut it off, and cast it from thee, for it is profitable for thee that one of thy members should perish, and not that thy whole body should be cast into hell.

Matthew 5:28-30 ⚔ All you devout Christian men who have sinned with your right hand while looking lustfully at a woman, please raise your only remaining hand.

Another of his disciples said to him, "Lord, allow me first to go and bury my father." But Jesus said to him, "Follow me, and **leave the dead to bury their own dead**."

Matthew 8:21-22 ⚔ Jesus had a strict no-funeral-leave policy.

ADVICE for those about to SACRIFICE

And the voice of the Lord came to Moses out of the Tent of meeting, saying, "Give these orders to the children of Israel: When anyone of you makes an offering to the Lord, you are to take it from the cattle, from the herd or from the flock. If the offering is a burned offering of the herd, let him give a male without a mark. He is to give it at the door of the Tent of meeting so that he may be pleasing to the Lord. And he is to put his hand on the head of the burned offering and it will be taken for him, to take away his sin. And the ox is to be put to death before the Lord. Then Aaron's sons, the priests, are to take the blood and put some of it on and round the altar which is at the door of the Tent of meeting. And the burned offering is to be skinned and cut up into its parts. And Aaron's sons, the priests, are to put fire on the altar and put the wood in order on the fire. And Aaron's sons, the priests, are to put the parts, the head and the fat, in order on the wood which is on the fire on the altar. But its inside parts and its legs are to be washed with water, and it will all be burned on the altar by the priest for a burned offering, an offering made by fire, for a sweet smell to the Lord.

> **Recipe for:** Sweet Smelling Burnt Ox
> **serves:** to take away sin
>
> Ingredients: 1 male ox (without mark)
> Directions: Preheat altar fire with ordered wood. Take ox to the door of the meeting tent, and place your hand on its head. Have ox put to death. Sprinkle blood around the altar. Cut up into parts and place head and fat parts on the fire. Wash inside parts and legs with water, then add to fire. Burn until you have made a sweet smell to the Lord.

"And if his offering is of the flock, a burned offering of sheep or goats, let him give a male without a mark. And he is to put it to death on the north side of the altar before the Lord. And Aaron's sons, the priests, are to put some of the blood on and round the altar. And the offering is to be cut into its parts, with its head and its fat, and the priest is to put them in order on the wood which is on the fire on the altar. But the inside parts and the legs are to be washed with water, and the priest will make an offering of all of it, burning it on the altar. It is a burned offering, an offering made by fire, for a sweet smell to the Lord.

"And if his offering to the Lord is a burned offering of birds, then he is to make his offering of doves or of young pigeons. And the priest is to take it to the altar, and after its head has been twisted off, it is to be burned on the altar, and its blood drained out on the side of the altar. And he is to take away its stomach, with its feathers, and put it down by the east side of the altar, where the burned waste is put. And let it be broken open at the wings,

> **Recipe for:** Young Pigeons with a Twist
> **serves:** The needs of Jehovah
>
> Ingredients: Young Pigeons - use as many as is required (may substitute doves)
> Directions: Take to the bird-head-twisting priest, who proceeds to take it to the altar and twist its head off. Be sure to drain its blood on the side of the altar. Remove stomach and feathers, discard. Gently break at wings and burn until sweet smelling.

but not cut in two, and let it be burned on the altar by the priest on the wood which is on the fire, it is a burned offering, an offering made by fire for a sweet smell to the Lord."

Leviticus 1

More Advice from Leviticus 2-4 🕮 "And when anyone makes a meal offering to the Lord, let his offering be of the best meal, with oil on it and perfume. And let him take it to Aaron's sons, the priests, and having taken in his hand some of the meal and of the oil, with all the perfume, let him give it to the priest to be burned on the altar, as a sign, an offering made by fire, for a sweet smell to the Lord. And the rest of the meal offering will be for Aaron and his sons. It is most holy among the Lord's fire offerings.

"And when you give a meal offering cooked in the oven, let it be of unleavened cakes of the best meal mixed with oil, or thin unleavened cakes covered with oil. And if you give a meal offering cooked on a flat plate, let it be of the best meal, unleavened and mixed with oil. Let it be broken into bits, and put oil on it; it is a meal offering. And if your offering is of meal cooked in fat over the fire, let it be made of the best meal mixed with oil. And you are to give the meal offering made of these things to the Lord, and let the priest take it to the altar. And he is to take from the meal offering a part, for a sign, burning it on the altar; an offering made by fire for a sweet smell to the Lord. And the rest of the meal offering will be for Aaron and his sons. It is most holy among the Lord's fire offerings.

"No meal offering which you give to the Lord is to be made with leaven; no leaven or honey is to be burned as an offering made by fire to the Lord. You may give them as an offering of first-fruits to the Lord, but they are not to go up as a sweet smell on the altar. And every meal offering is to be salted with salt; your meal offering is not to be without the salt of the agreement of your God. With all your offerings give salt.

"And if you give a meal offering of first-fruits to the Lord, give, as your offering of first-fruits, new grain, made dry with fire, crushed new grain. And put oil on it and perfume. It is a meal offering. And part of the meal of the offering and part of the oil and all the perfume is to be burned for a sign by the priest. It is an offering made by fire to the Lord.

"And if his offering is given for a peace-offering, if he gives of the herd, male or female, let him give it without any mark on it, before the Lord. And he is to put his hand on the head of his offering and put it to death at the door of the Tent of meeting, and Aaron's sons, the priests, are to put some of the blood on and round the altar. And he is to give of the peace-offering, as an offering made by fire to the Lord; the fat covering the inside parts and all the fat on the inside parts, and the two kidneys, and the fat on them, which is by the top part of the legs, and the fat joining the liver and the kidneys, he is to take away, that it may be burned by Aaron's sons on the altar, on the burned offering which is on the wood on the fire: it is an offering made by fire of a sweet smell to the Lord. And if what he gives for a peace-offering to the Lord is of the flock, let him give a male or female, without any mark on it. If his offering is a lamb, then let it be placed before the Lord.

🕮 *Bible Funmentionables'* Handy **SIN & SACRIFICE Summary**	
Sin	Sacrifice
Wrongdoing by a chief priest or by the people of Israel	An **ox**
Wrongdoing by a ruler	A **goat**
Wrongdoing by the common people	A **goat** or **lamb**
Failing to testify under oath, unintentionally touching something unclean, or thoughtlessly taking an oath for good or evil	A **goat** or **lamb** If not a goat, then **two doves**. If not two doves, then a tenth of an ephah of **fine flour** (with no oil and no perfume on it)
Failing to offer first fruits or tithes which are due to the priests	A **sheep** of proper value and pay **120% of restitution**

And he is to put his hand on the head of his offering and put it to death before the Tent of meeting, and Aaron's sons are to put some of its blood on and round the altar. And of the peace-offering, let him give an offering made by fire to the Lord, the fat of it, all the fat tail, he is to take away near the backbone, and the fat covering the inside parts and all the fat on the inside parts, And the two kidneys, with the fat on them, which is by the top part of the legs, and the fat joining the liver and the kidneys, he is to take away, that it may be burned by the priest on the altar; it is the food of the offering made by fire to the Lord.

"And if his offering is a goat, then let it be placed before the Lord, And let him put his hand on the head of it and put it to death before the Tent of meeting; and the sons of Aaron are to put some of its blood on and round the altar. And of it let him make his offering, an offering made by fire to the Lord; the fat covering the inside parts and all the fat on the inside parts, and the two kidneys, with the fat on them, which is by the top part of the legs, and the fat joining the liver and the kidneys, let him take away, that it may be burned by the priest on the altar; it is the food of the offering made by fire for a sweet smell: all the fat is the Lord's. Let it be an order forever, through all your generations, in all your houses, that you are not to take fat or blood for food."

And the Lord said to Moses, "Say to the children of Israel: These are the offerings of anyone who does wrong through error, doing any of the things which by the Lord's order are not to be done: If the chief priest by doing wrong becomes a cause of sin to the people, then let him give to the Lord for the sin which he has done, an ox, without any mark, for a sin-offering. And he is to take the ox to the door of the Tent of meeting before the Lord, and put his hand on its head and put it to death before the Lord. And the chief priest is to take some of its blood and take it to the Tent of meeting, and the priest is to put his finger in the blood, shaking drops of it before the Lord seven times, in front of the veil of the holy place. And the priest is to put some of the blood on the horns of the altar on which perfume is burned before the Lord in the Tent of meeting, draining out all the rest of the blood of the ox at the base of the altar of burned offering which is at the door of the Tent of meeting. And he is to take away all the fat of the ox of the sin-offering; the fat covering the inside parts and all the fat of the inside parts, And the two kidneys, with the fat on them, which is by the top part of the legs, and the fat joining the liver and the kidneys, he is to take away, as it is taken from the ox of the peace-offering; and it is to be burned by the priest on the altar of burned offerings. And the skin of the ox and all its flesh, with its head and its legs and its inside parts and its waste, all the ox, he is to take away outside the circle of the tents into a clean place where the burned waste is put, and there it is to be burned on wood with fire.

"And if all the people of Israel do wrong, without anyone's knowledge; if they have done any of the things which by the Lord's order are not to be done, causing sin to come on them; when the sin which they have done comes to light, then let all the people give an ox for a sin-offering, and take it before the Tent of meeting. And let the chiefs of the people put their hands on its head before the Lord, and put the ox to death before the Lord. And the priest is to take some of its blood to the Tent of meeting; and put his finger in the blood, shaking drops of the blood seven times before the Lord in front of the veil. And he is to put some of the blood on the horns of the altar which is before the Lord in the Tent of meeting; and all the rest of the blood is to be drained out at the base of the altar of burned offering at the door of the Tent of meeting. And he is to take off all its fat, burning it on the altar. Let him do with the ox as he did with the ox of the sin-offering; and the priest will take away their sin and they will have forgiveness. Then let the ox be taken away outside the tent-circle, that it may be burned as the other ox was burned; it is the sin-offering for all the people.

"If a ruler does wrong, and in error does any of the things which, by the order of the Lord his God, are not to be done, causing sin to come on him; when the sin which he has done is made clear to him, let him give for his offering a goat, a male without any mark. And he is to put his hand on the head of the goat and put it to death in the place where they put to death the burned offering before the Lord: it is a sin-offering. And the priest is to take some of the blood of the offering with his finger and put it on the horns of the altar of burned offering, draining out the rest of the blood at the base of the altar of burned offering. And all the fat of it is to be burned on the altar like the fat of the peace-offering; and the priest will take away his sin and he will have forgiveness. And if any one of the common people does wrong in error, doing any of the things which the Lord has given orders are not to be done, causing sin to come on him . . .

GOOD ADVICE

Don't get the wrong idea that the Bible contains only bad advice. Amidst all the questionable quotations, you can find some good, common-sense advice every so often. Disappointingly though, you can almost always find a different passage that contradicts the sensible one.

Thou shalt not curse the deaf, nor put a **stumbling block before the blind**, but thou shalt fear the Lord thy God, because I am the Lord.
Leviticus 19:14 ☝ *Don't curse the lip-reading deaf anyway.*

Neither shall he multiply wives to himself, that his heart turn not away. Neither shall he greatly multiply to himself silver and gold.
Deuteronomy 17:17 ☝ *And having multiple ex-wives can divide you from your silver and gold.*

Thou shalt not deliver unto his master **the servant which is escaped** from his master unto thee.
Deuteronomy 23:15 ☝ *Though mostly pro-slavery, the Bible does cut a little slack to the escaped slave.*

And the angel of the Lord appeared to the woman, and said to her, "Behold, now, thou art barren and bearest not, but thou shalt conceive and bear a son. Now therefore beware, I pray thee, and **drink not wine nor strong drink**, and eat not any unclean thing."
Judges 13:3-4 ☝ *A fetal alcohol syndrome warning in the Bible.*

Happy is the man that **findeth wisdom** and the man that getteth understanding.
Proverbs 3:13 ☝ *Being wise may not bring you 300 concubines like wise old Solomon had, but it may bring you some happiness.*

A false balance is abomination to the Lord, but a just weight **is his delight**.
Proverbs 11:1 ☝ *Assuming you make it to heaven, God will certainly compliment you on your just weight. Just wait.*

The simple man believes everything, but the prudent man **carefully considers his ways**.
Proverbs 14:15 Is the Bible saying, *"Don't believe everything you read?"*

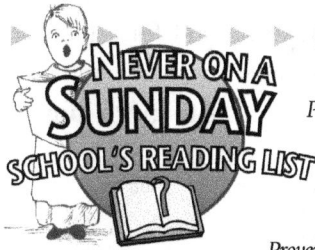

NEVER ON A SUNDAY SCHOOL'S READING LIST

The poor man is hated even by his neighbor, but the man of **wealth has numbers of friends**.
Proverbs 14:20

Wealth makes a great number of friends, but the poor man is parted from his friend.
Proverbs 19:4 It's hard to deny that there is some truth to this.

A merry heart maketh **a cheerful countenance**.
Proverbs 15:13 But what makes a merry heart?

PITY THE TRANSLATOR 4

If you've ever been camping in the wild, you know about the "necessities of nature," but how do you mention it in the bestselling book of all-time? Below is the Douay-Rheims translation followed by other options to choose from.

Thou shalt have a place without the camp, to which thou mayst go for the **necessities of nature**, carrying a paddle at thy girdle. And when thou sittest down, thou shalt dig round about, and with the earth that is dug up thou shalt cover.
Deuteronomy 23:12-13

And thou shalt have a paddle among thy weapons...

and it shall be when thou wilt **ease thyself abroad**, thou shalt dig with it, and shalt turn back, and cover that which cometh from thee. *Webster's*

and it hath been, **in thy sitting without**, that thou hast digged with it, and turned back, and covered thy filth. *Young's Literal Translation*

and it shall be, when thou wilt **ease thyself abroad**, thou shalt dig therewith, and shalt turn back and cover that which cometh from thee. *King James Version*

and it shall be, when thou **sittest down abroad**, thou shalt dig therewith, and shalt turn back and cover that which is come from thee. *Darby Translation*

and it shall be, when you **sit down abroad**, you shall dig therewith, and shall turn back and cover that which comes from you. *World English Bible*

and when you have **been to that place**, let that which comes from you be covered up with earth. *Bible in Basic English*

He that loveth silver shall **not be satisfied with silver**, nor he that loveth abundance with increase. This is also vanity.

Ecclesiastes 5:10 📖 *Good advice that never seems to get through to some people.*

Therefore **I commended mirth**, because there was no good for a man under the sun, but to eat, and drink, and be merry, and that he should take nothing else with him of his labor in the days of his life, which God hath given him under the sun.

Ecclesiastes 8:15 📖 *Translation: You can't take it with you, so why not just enjoy what you've got while you still can.*

If the clouds are full of rain, they empty themselves on the earth, and if a tree falls toward the south, or toward the north, in the place where the tree falls, **there shall it be**.

Ecclesiastes 11:3 📖 *It may be a little obvious, but it's undeniably true.*

When you pray, **you shall not be as the hypocrites**, for they love to stand and pray in the synagogues and in the corners of the streets, that they may be seen by men. Most certainly, I tell you, they have received their reward.

Matthew 6:5 📖 *Not a favorite of the prayer-in-public-schools folks.*

UNSAFE PASSAGE
Unsuitable for Student-Led Prayer

Judge not, that ye be not judged.

Matthew 7:1 📖 *Sounds easier than it is.*

All those things which you would have men **do unto you**, even so do you to them, because this is the law and the prophets.

Matthew 7:12 📖 *Jesus wasn't the first to promote the Golden Rule, but what self-respecting religion doesn't have their version of it?*

The Bible in Headlines

Jesus recommends securing adequate funding before starting construction
Otherwise risk public ridicule, adds Nazarene

JERUSALEM, Judea - For which of you, desiring to **put up a tower**, does not first give much thought to the price, if he will have enough to make it complete? For fear that if he makes a start and is not able to go on with it to the end, all who see it will be laughing at him and saying, "This man made a start at building and is not able to make it complete."

Luke 14:28-30 📖 *This is straight out of the State Contractors Licensing Board Test.*

At midnight Paul and Silas prayed and sang praises unto God, and the prisoners heard them. And suddenly there was a great earthquake, so that the foundations of the prison were shaken, and immediately **all the doors were opened**, and everyone's bands were loosed. And the keeper of the prison awaking out of his sleep and seeing the prison doors open, he drew out his sword and would have killed himself, supposing that the prisoners had been fled. But Paul cried with a loud voice, saying, "Do thyself no harm, for we are all here."

Acts 16:25-28 ⚏ The worthwhile lesson here is not that you should expect an earthquake to free you from jail, but rather this is a warning to avoid making any rash decisions to commit suicide.

I have shown you all things, how that so laboring ye ought to support the weak and to remember the words of the Lord Jesus, how he said, "***It is more blessed to give than to receive***."

Acts 20:35 ⚏ This Jesus quote is memorable to us, but it wasn't very memorable to the Gospel writers as it never appears in any of the gospels.

Rejoice with them that do rejoice, and weep with them that weep. Be of the same mind one toward another. Mind not high things, but condescend to men of low estate. Be not wise in your own conceits. Recompense to no man evil for evil. Provide things honest in the sight of all men. If it be possible, as much as lieth in you, ***live peaceably with all men***.

Romans 12:15-18 ⚏ Besides, it can be a little awkward to be rejoicing with the weeping.

Now accept one ***who is weak in faith***, but not for disputes over opinions.

Romans 14:1 ⚏ It's refreshing to find the word "accept" in the Bible, where it refers to a person and isn't preceded by the word "not."

I robbed other churches, taking wages of them that I might minister unto you.

2 Corinthians 11:8 ⚏ Following Paul's holy example, many televangelists raise money by promising to spread their ministry to others, though most fail to follow Paul's example of labeling it robbery.

Let us not be desirous of vain glory, provoking one another, envying one another.

Galatians 5:26

Fathers, ***provoke not your children to anger***, lest they be discouraged.

Colossians 3:21 ⚏ Provocative passages about not being provocative.

Beware of dogs, beware of evil workers, beware of the concision.

Philippians 3:2 ⚏ And beware of evil dogs especially.

BIBLE ANALYSIS MADE EASY

⚏ In your religious studies, if you ever have to choose a Bible verse to analyze, it doesn't get much easier than Job 3:2, printed in its entirety below.

"And he said."

Now we exhort you, brethren, warn them that are unruly, comfort the feebleminded, support the weak, be patient toward all men. See that none render evil for evil unto any man, but **ever follow that which is good**, both among yourselves and to all men.

1 Thessalonians 5:14-15 Be patient toward all men, including those who like to quote from the Bible Funmentionables' "Bad Advice" chapter.

For even when we were with you, this we commanded you, that if any would not work, **neither should he eat**.

2 Thessalonians 3:10 Sounds like many parents at chore time.

For we brought nothing into this world, and it is certain we can carry nothing out. And having food and raiment, with these **let us be content**.

Timothy 6:7-8 Having food and water is better than having nothing, but yet not quite as cool as having food and water and a dune buggy.

But **avoid foolish questions, and genealogies**, and contentions, and strivings about the law, for they are unprofitable and vain.

Titus 3:9 After you've read all the way through until the very end of the Bible, it tells you to avoid genealogies. This belongs in the Bible's preface.

For when God made his promise to Abraham, because he could swear by no greater, **he swore by himself.**

Hebrews 6:13 God and I have so much in common. When I'm working alone on a difficult home improvement project, I swear by myself, and I usually use his name when I do.

For it is not possible that **the blood of bulls and of goats** should take away sins.

Hebrews 10:4 After sacrificing the lives of untold thousands of bulls and goats, now we're told that it really had no effect whatsoever. Maybe it's best not to contemplate the many children who needlessly lost beloved pet goats during all those years.

Be not forgetful to **entertain strangers**, for thereby some have entertained angels unawares.

Hebrews 13:2 Good advice for strangers wanting to be entertained: throw subtle hints into the conversation that could lead your potential host to conclude that you may just be an angel.

Be not carried about with various and strange doctrines. For it is a good thing that the heart be established with grace, **not with meats**, which have not profited them that have been occupied therein.
Hebrews 13:9 ⚰ *Modern research proves the Bible to be true: too much of certain meats are bad for your heart.*

Pure and undefiled religion before God and the Father is this: to **visit orphans and widows** in their affliction, to keep oneself unspotted from the world.
James 1:27 ⚰ *It's not about attending the right church, reciting the one true creed, and dropping the correct amount in the collection plate?*

For if there come unto your assembly a man with a gold ring, in goodly apparel, and there come in also a poor man in vile raiment, and ye have **respect to him that weareth the gay clothing**, and say unto him, "Sit thou here in a good place," and say to the poor, "Stand thou there, or sit here under my footstool," are ye not then partial in yourselves and are become judges of evil thoughts?
James 2:2-4 ⚰ *In my youth, when I would wear gay clothing, I got less respect than you would think.*

Whereas you don't know what your life will be like tomorrow. **For what is your life? For you are a vapor**, that appears for a little time and then vanishes away.
James 4:14 ⚰ *Easy for you to say; you've been dead 2,000 years!*

My loved ones, do not put your faith in every spirit, but **put them to the test**, to see if they are from God, because a great number of false prophets have gone out into the world.
1 John 4:1 ⚰ *Maybe have them do the poison-drinking test (Mark 16:18).*

Jesus said, "You can't enter the strong man's house and do him harm without **tying his hands**. Only then can you loot his house."

Jesus said, "The Father's kingdom is like unto a person who wanted to **kill a powerful person**. While in his house, he drew his sword and stabbed it into the wall to see if his hand would be strong enough. Then he went and killed the powerful one."
Gospel of Thomas #35 & #98 ⚰ *With advice like this, how many convicts wish they had found Jesus before going to prison.*

CONTRADICTIONS

Inconsistencies abound in any book that's been written by scores of authors over the course of a thousand years—and then translated and mistranslated, and then copied and miscopied. There is some truth in advertising: it isn't called the Flawless Book, but rather, more humbly, the Good Book.

But of the tree of knowledge of good and evil thou shalt not eat of it, for in the day that thou eatest thereof **thou shalt surely die**.

Genesis 2:17

———— & ————

And all the days that Adam lived were **nine hundred and thirty years**, and he died.

Genesis 5:5 🕮 *"Thou shalt surely" roughly translates to "whenever I get around to it."*

And the Lord said to Cain, "Where is your brother Abel?" And he said, "I have no idea. Am I my brother's keeper?" And he said, "What have you done? The voice of your brother's blood is crying to me from the earth. And now you are cursed from the earth, whose mouth is open to take your brother's blood from your hand. No longer will the earth give you her fruit as the reward of your work. **You will be a wanderer in flight over the earth**."

Genesis 4:9-12

———— & ————

And Cain went away from before the face of the Lord and made his living place in the land of Nod on the east of Eden. And Cain knoweth his wife, and she conceiveth, and beareth Enoch. And **he is building a city**, and he calleth the name of the city Enoch, according to the name of his son.

Genesis 4:16-17 🕮 *For a guy who was cursed from the earth, he sure seemed to do a lot of building, and knowething, and conceivething.*

BENJAMIN'S 3 TO 10 SONS

🕮 The guy with the coat of many colors also had the genealogy of many variations. Genesis 46:21 lists ten sons, while 1 Chronicles 8:1-2 mentions five sons, and 1 Chronicles 7:6 contains only three sons. This list does have some value, as it reveals the worst possible names to give to twins: Huppim and Muppim.

Genesis 46:21	**1 Chronicles 7:6**
Ard	Becher
Ashbel	Bela
Becher	Jediael
Belah	
Ehi	**1 Chronicles 8:1-2**
Gera	Aharah
Huppim	Ashbel
Muppim	Bela
Naaman	Nohah
Rosh	Rapha

Of every living thing of all flesh, **two of every sort** shalt thou bring into the ark.

Genesis 6:19

——— & ———

Of every clean beast you will **take seven males and seven females**, and of the beasts which are not clean, two, the male and his female.

Genesis 7:2 📖 *"Wait, wait, the original contract clearly states that I only had to find two of each animal. Let me talk to your supervisor."*

THE UNTOLD STORY
The Deleted Details from Popular Passages

And he said, "Take now thy son, **thine only son Isaac**, whom thou lovest, and get thee into the land of Moriah, and offer him there for a burnt offering upon one of the mountains which I will tell thee of."

Genesis 22:2

——— & ———

Then again Abraham took a wife, and her name was Keturah. And **she bare him Zimran, Jokshan, Medan, Midian, Ishbak, and Shuah**.

Genesis 25:1-2 📖 *Back in the day, you wanted to have more than one son just in case the Lord commanded you bump one off.*

And God said unto him, "Thy name is Jacob. Thy name shall not be called any more Jacob, but **Israel shall be thy name**," and he called his name Israel.

Genesis 35:10

——— & ———

And God spake unto Israel in the visions of the night and said, "**Jacob, Jacob**." And he said, "Here am I."

Genesis 46:2 📖 *Remember, Jacob, your new name is Israel. OK, Jacob?*

And Moses said unto the Lord, "O my Lord, **I am not eloquent**, neither heretofore, nor since thou hast spoken unto thy servant, but I am slow of speech and of a slow tongue."

Exodus 4:10

——— & ———

And Moses was learned in all the wisdom of the Egyptians and was **mighty in words** and in deeds.

Acts 7:22 📖 *When you have King James' most esteemed scholars translating your words, you come across as being eloquent even when complaining of not being eloquent.*

MULTIPLE CREATION DISORDER

BIBLE FUNMENTIONABLE QUIZ

Making order out of chaos isn't easy, especially if you have to create the universe twice, in two different ways. Arrange the words below in the order they were created.

Genesis Chapter 1

Firmament	1	
Birds	2	
Light	3	
Earth	4	
Plants	5	
Stars	6	
Heaven	7	
Animals	8	
Sun	9	
Fish	10	
Moon	11	
People	12	
Heaven	13	

Genesis Chapter 2

Eden	1	
Woman	2	
Heaven	3	
Man	4	
Earth	5	
Animals	6	

Genesis 1: Heaven, Earth, Light, Firmament, Plants, Sun, Moon, Stars, Fish, Birds, Animals, People

Genesis 2: Heaven, Earth, Man, Garden of Eden, Animals, Woman

Thou shalt not bow down thyself to them, nor serve them, for I the Lord thy God am a jealous God, **visiting the iniquity of the fathers upon the children** to the third and fourth generation of them that hate me.

Exodus 20:5

&

Fathers are not to be put to death for their children or children for their fathers. **Every man is to be put to death for the sin which he himself has done**.

Deuteronomy 24:16 ⚖ A leap forward in criminal justice history that we all take for granted: not punishing a criminal's great-grandchildren.

Thou shalt not **speak ill of the gods**, and the ruler of thy people thou shalt not curse.

Exodus 22:28

&

Remember the former things of old, for I am God, and **there is none else**. I am God, and there is none like me.

Isaiah 46:9 ⚖ Jehovah is so jealous of the other gods (that we later find out don't exist) that he orders his followers to kill those who worship other gods—but in a surprising twist we're not allowed to speak ill of them.

And again the Lord said, "Behold there is a place near me, and thou shalt stand upon the rock. And when my glory shall pass by, I will set thee in a hole of the rock, and protect thee with my right hand, till I pass. And I will take away my hand, and **thou shalt see my back parts**, but my face thou canst not see."

Exodus 33:20-23

UNSAFE PASSAGE
Unsuitable for Student-Led Prayer

&

No man has seen God at any time. The only Son, who is on the breast of the Father, he has made clear what God is.

John 1:18 ⚖ Moses may not be the only person to get a rear view of God. Jacob could easily have gotten a glance when he spent all night wrestling against God. (Genesis 32:24-30) God wasn't powerful enough to beat him, but he was able to touch Jacob's thigh and dislocate it, thus preserving God's undefeated wrestling record.

Thou shalt **love the Lord** thy God with thy whole heart, and with thy whole soul, and with thy whole strength.

Deuteronomy 6:5

&

Thou shalt **fear the Lord** thy God, and serve him, and shalt swear by his name.

Deuteronomy 6:13

&

There is no fear in love. True love has no room for fear, because where fear is, there is pain, and he who is not free from fear is not complete in love.

1 John 4:18 ⚖ Or you could love the Lord on Sunday through Tuesday and fear the Lord on Thursday through Saturday and alternate Wednesdays.

Behold, the heaven and the heaven of heavens is **the Lord's thy God**, the earth also, with all that is therein.

Deuteronomy 10:14

——— & ———

The heaven, even the heavens, are the Lord's, but the earth hath he given to **the children of men**.

Psalms 115:16 ⚰ *If the Lord already owns heaven and the heaven of heavens, why would he also want to be landlord for such troublesome tenants on earth? What with our droughts and floods, our icestorms and firestorms, our starvation and obesity, our* Teen Wolf *and* Teen Wolf Too.

Cursed be the man that **maketh any graven or molten image**, an abomination unto the Lord, the work of the hands of the craftsman.

Deuteronomy 27:15

——— & ———

You shall **make two cherubim of hammered gold**. You shall make them at the two ends of the mercy seat.

Exodus 25:18 ⚰ *But it's an adorable abomination.*

Wherefore then do ye harden your hearts, as **the Egyptians and Pharaoh hardened their hearts**?

1 Samuel 6:6

——— & ———

But the **Lord hardened Pharaoh's heart**, so that he would not let the children of Israel go.

Exodus 10:20 ⚰ *Who among us, if we were writing back then, could have avoided the temptation to ever so slightly rewrite the history of this story?*

David put his hand in his bag, and took a stone, and slang it, and smote the Philistine in his forehead, that the stone sunk into his forehead, and he fell upon his face to the earth. David prevailed over the Philistine with a sling and with a stone, and smote the Philistine, and slew him, but **there was no sword** in the hand of David.

1 Samuel 17:49-50

——— & ———

David ran, and stood upon the Philistine, and **took his sword**, and drew it out of the sheath thereof, and slew him, and cut off his head therewith.

1 Samuel 17:51 ⚰ *Though not proof that Goliath was actually one guy on another guy's shoulders, having to slay him twice is a giant tip-off.*

Therefore **Saul took a sword and fell upon it**. So Saul died.

1 Samuel 31:4-6

——— & ———

And David went and took the bones of Saul and the bones of Jonathan his son from the men of Jabeshgilead, which had stolen them from the street of Bethshan, where the Philistines had hanged them, when **the Philistines had slain Saul** in Gilboa.

2 Samuel 21:12 ⚰ *Was Saul the type to try to make his suicide look like a murder? Serious Bible detectives can find further complications to the mystery in 2 Samuel 1:8-10 and 1 Chronicles 10:14.*

These are the names of David's mighty warriors: Ishbaal the Hachmonite, chief of the three. He raised his spear against **eight hundred men**, whom he killed in one encounter.

2 Samuel 23:8

——— & ———

This is the list of David's men of war: Ishbaal, the son of a Hachmonite, chief of the three. He raised his spear against **three hundred men**, whom he killed in one encounter.

1 Chronicles 11:11 ⚊ *Who really expects accuracy when counting the other side's casualties?*

There was **nothing in the ark save the two tables** which Moses put therein at Horeb, when the Lord made a covenant with the children of Israel, when they came out of Egypt.

2 Chronicles 5:10

——— & ———

The ark of the covenant overlaid round about with gold, wherein was **the golden pot that had manna, and Aaron's rod** that budded, and the tables of the covenant.

Hebrews 9:4 ⚊ *Never having owned a golden pot, it's hard to know if that's the best way to store bread from heaven.*

The children of Bezai, **three hundred twenty three**.

Ezra 2:17

——— & ———

The children of Bezai, **three hundred twenty four**.

Nehemiah 7:23 ⚊ *If they knew they'd be criticized for inaccuracy a few millennia later, they probably would have checked their numbers just one more time.*

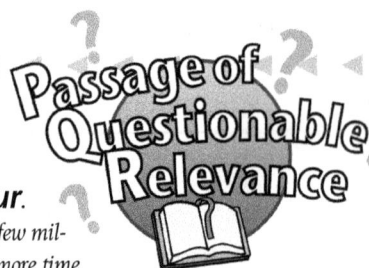

Passage of Questionable Relevance

Besides their men-servants and their maid-servants, of whom there were seven thousand three hundred thirty and seven, and they had **two hundred singing men and women**.

Ezra 2:65

——— & ———

Beside their men-servants and their maid-servants, of whom there were seven thousand three hundred thirty and seven, and they had **two hundred forty and five singing men and women**.

Nehemiah 7:67 ⚊ *An accurate count of servants is obviously more important than knowing exactly how many choir members you have.*

EGYPT'S UNKILLABLE CATTLE (& HORSES)

The fifth plague clearly states that all of Egypt's cattle died, and it suggests that all the horses died too. However, soon afterwards the zombie cattle rise up and need to be plagued to death two more times, and the undead horses all drown chasing the Israelites through the parted Red Sea.

Plague 5: Behold, the hand of Jehovah shall be on thy **cattle** which is in the field, on the **horses**, on the asses, on the camels, on the oxen and on the sheep, with a very grievous plague. And Jehovah did this thing on the following day, and **all the cattle of Egypt died**, but of the cattle of the children of Israel died not one. *Exodus 9:3,6*

The righteous shall **rejoice** when he seeth the vengeance. He shall wash his feet in the blood of the wicked.

Psalms 58:10

——— & ———

Rejoice not when thine enemy falleth, and let not thine heart be glad when he stumbleth.

Proverbs 24:17 🔖 *Nobody said following the Bible was easy. Many righteous people would rather not wash their feet in blood, and they do in fact let their hearts be a little glad when their enemy stumbles.*

When a man's ways please the Lord, he maketh even his enemies to **be at peace with him**.

Proverbs 16:7

——— & ———

All that will live godly in Christ Jesus **shall suffer persecution**.

2 Timothy 3:12 🔖 *If your enemies are the top-notch, arch-enemy types, they are actually able to be at peace while they persecute you.*

Whoso findeth a wife **findeth a good thing** and obtaineth favor of the Lord.

Proverbs 18:22

——— & ———

It is good for a man **not to touch a woman**.

1 Corinthians 7:1 🔖 *In some circumstances, Paul is completely right! For example, men should not touch a woman with smallpox, a waitress carrying drinks, or a police-woman who is pulling you over to give you a speeding ticket. Inspirational words to live by, if you just know the correct interpretation.*

UNLIKELY SIGN
From a Fan in the Stands

1 Corinthians 7:1

Don't Touch Women

Go and proclaim these words toward the north. Thou shalt say, "'Return, O rebellious Israel,' saith the Lord, 'and I will not turn away my face from you. For I am holy,' saith the Lord, 'and **I will not be angry forever**.'"

Jeremiah 3:12

——— & ———

And of thyself thou shalt let go thine inheritance which I gave thee, and I will cause thee to serve thine enemies in a land that thou knowest not. For ye have kindled a fire in **mine anger, it shall burn forever**.

Jeremiah 17:4 🔖 *A little good cop/bad cop action from on high.*

Plague 7: Send therefore now, and gather thy **cattle**, and all that thou hast in the field; for upon every man and beast which shall be found in the field, and shall not be brought home, the hail shall come down upon them, and **they shall die**. Exodus 9:19

Plague 10: And it came to pass, that at midnight **the Lord smote** all the firstborn in the land of Egypt, from the firstborn of Pharaoh that sat on his throne unto the firstborn of the captive that was in the dungeon, and all the firstborn of **cattle**. Exodus 12:29

Red Sea Chase: And the Egyptians pursued and came after them, **all Pharaoh's horses**, his chariots and his horsemen, into the midst of the sea. Exodus 14:23

And you will **take your oath**, by the living Lord, in good faith and wisdom and righteousness. And the nations will make use of you as a blessing, and in you will they take pride.
Jeremiah 4:2

———— & ————

But above all things, brethren, **swear not**, neither by heaven, neither by the earth, neither by any other oath. But let your yea be yea, and your nay, nay, lest ye fall into condemnation.
James 5:12 📖 *And while we're at it, let your no be no, your whoa, whoa, and your hey, hey, and your my, my, and your rock and roll can never die.*

Behold, I am the Lord, the God of all flesh. **Is there any thing too hard for the Lord?**
Jeremiah 32:27

———— & ————

And the Lord was with Judah, and he drove out the inhabitants of the mountain, but **could not drive out** the inhabitants of the valley, because they had chariots of iron.
Judges 1:19 📖 *Either the Lord or Judah needed to invest in an anti-iron-chariot weapon system.*

Even so **let your light shine** before men, that they may see your good works, and glorify your Father who is in heaven.
Matthew 5:16

———— & ————

Take heed that ye **do not your righteousness before men**, to be seen of them, else ye have no reward with your Father who is in heaven.
Matthew 6:1 📖 *You can really please God by letting your light shine and hoping that no one is looking.*

LISTING APOSTLES
11 OUT OF 12 AIN'T BAD

📖 Is it really all that important to know every single name in Jesus' band of followers? It's just the important names that matter—like the way most people can name only one or two members of the Jackson 5 or Bob Marley & the Wailers.

Matthew's Gospel	Luke's Gospel
Andrew	Andrew
Bartholomew	Bartholomew
James	James
James	James
John	John
Judas Iscariot	Judas Iscariot
Matthew	Matthew
Philip	Philip
Simon Peter	Simon Peter
Simon the Canaanite	Simon Zeolotes
Thomas	Thomas
Lebbaeus Thaddeus	Judas (James' brother)

These twelve Jesus sent forth, and commanded them, saying, "**Go not into the way of the Gentiles**, and into any city of the Samaritans enter ye not. But go rather to the lost sheep of the house of Israel."
Matthew 10:5-6

———— & ————

Go ye therefore and **teach all nations**, baptizing them in the name of the Father, and of the Son, and of the Holy Ghost.
Matthew 28:19 📖 *The marketing strategy begins.*

He that is not with me is **against me**, and he that gathereth not with me scattereth abroad.
Matthew 12:30

———— & ————

He who is not against us is **for us**.
Mark 9:40 📖 *So technically the people who don't take a side are both for and against Jesus.*

Except ye be converted, and **become as little children**, ye shall not enter into the kingdom of heaven.

Matthew 18:3

——— & ———

When I was a child, I spake as a child, I understood as a child, I thought as a child. But when I became a man, *I put away childish things*.

1 Corinthians 13:11 🔏 *Maybe it's best to try to get into the kingdom of heaven while you are still a child, and aren't expected to put away childish things just yet.*

And he said that they were to take nothing for their journey, but **a stick only**. No bread, no bag, no money in their pockets. They were to go with common shoes on their feet, and not to take two coats.

Mark 6:8-9

——— & ———

And he said to them, "Take nothing for your journey, **no stick** or bag or bread or money, and do not take two coats."

Luke 9:3 🔏 *Sounds like wearing two coats was all the rage back then, and the one thing you really shouldn't do.*

And he was very sad in spirit and said, "Why is this generation looking for a sign? Truly, I say to you, **no sign will be given** to this generation."

Mark 8:12

——— & ———

"And **there will be signs** in the sun and moon and stars and on the earth, fear among the nations and doubt because of the loud noise of the sea and the waves. And then will they see the Son of Man coming in a cloud with great power and glory. Verily I say to you, this generation shall not pass away, till all be fulfilled."

Luke 21:25,27,32 🔏 *No wonder so many Christians think Jesus is coming back in their lifetime: Jesus did say it would happen before the end of "this generation."*

PITY THE TRANSLATOR 5

Nehemiah is surveying Jerusalem to rebuild the city's wall in Nehemiah 2:13. How hard can that be to translate?

❝ And I went out by night by the gate of the valley, even before **the dragon well, and to the dung port**, and viewed the walls of Jerusalem, which were broken down, and the gates thereof were consumed with fire.

– *King James Bible*

❝ And I went out by night by the gate of the valley, and before **the dragon fountain, and to the dung gate**.

– *Douay-Rheims Bible*

❝ And I went out by night by the valley-gate, even toward **the jackal-fountain, and to the dung-gate**.

– *Darby Bible Translation*

❝ I went out by night by the valley gate, even toward **the jackal's well, and to the dung gate**.

– *World English Bible*

❝ And I went out by night, through the doorway of the valley, and past **the dragon's water-spring as far as the place where waste material was put**.

– *Bible in Basic English*

And Jesus asked him saying, "What is thy name?" And he said, "Legion," for many demons had entered into him. And they besought him that he would not command them to go away ***into the bottomless pit***.

Luke 8:30-31

—— & ——

And he asked him, "What is thy name?" And he saith to him, "My name is Legion, for we are many." And he besought him much, that he would not drive him away ***out of the country***.

Mark 5:9-10 ⚰ If given the choice, the bottomless pit does sound exciting, but traveling abroad gets my vote.

(And the Lord said,) "***You fools***, did not he that made the outside make the inside also?"

Luke 11:40

—— & ——

But I tell you, that whoever is angry with his brother shall be in danger of the judgment. And whoever says to his brother, "Raca," shall be in danger of the council. But whosoever shall say, "You fool!" ***shall be in danger of hell fire***.

Matthew 5:22 ⚰ Technically, Jesus did say "You fools," not "You fool" in the first quote, so he should be safe from hell fire. He was no raca (lamebrain).

And they brought him to Jesus, and they cast their garments upon the ***colt***, and they set Jesus thereon.

Luke 19:35

—— & ——

And Jesus, when he had found a young ***ass***, sat thereon, as it is written.

John 12:14 ⚰ Either way, he was traveling in style.

And they said to them, "The Lord is risen indeed, and hath appeared to Simon." And they told what things were done in the way, and how he was known of them in breaking of bread. And as they thus spake, Jesus himself stood in the midst of them, and saith unto them, "Peace be unto you." But they were ***terrified and affrighted***, and supposed that they had seen a spirit. And he said unto them, "Why are ye troubled? and why do thoughts arise in your hearts?"

Luke 24:34-38

—— & ——

Then the same day at evening, being the first day of the week, when the doors were shut, where the disciples were assembled for fear of the Jews, came Jesus and stood in the midst, and saith unto them, "Peace be unto you." After his resurrection, Jesus could walk through walls. And when he had so said, he showed unto them his hands and his side. Then were the disciples ***glad***, when they saw the Lord.

John 20:19-20 ⚰ Their resurrected friend can walk through walls, so you might expect them to be glad—and a little terrified.

And **no one has ever gone up** to heaven but he who came down from heaven, the Son of Man.

John 3:13

——— & ———

And **Elijah went up** by a whirlwind into heaven.

2 Kings 2:11 ☙ *To John, whirlwind-assisted ascensions don't count as true ascensions.*

After these things came Jesus and his disciples into the land of Judaea, and there he abode with them and **baptized**.

John 3:22

——— & ———

However Jesus himself **baptized not**, but his disciples.

John 4:2 ☙ *To b. or not to b.?*

You heard me say to you, "I am going away, and yet I am coming to you." If you loved me, you would have rejoiced because I am going to the Father, for **the Father is greater than I am**.

John 14:28

——— & ———

I and my Father are one.

John 10:30 ☙ *He's coming, he's going, he's greater, he's the same. A good messiah is a lot of things to a lot of people.*

BIBLE FUNMENTIONABLES QUIZ

Bible Funmentionables'
EASIEST MULTIPLE CHOICE TEST EVER

☙ **Choose from the options below.**

1. The Lord is a	**A.** Man of war **B.** God of peace
2. Joseph was the son of	**A.** Jacob **B.** Heli
3. Are all sins forgivable?	**A.** Yes **B.** No
4. How many stalls for horses and chariots did Solomon have?	**A.** 40,000 **B.** 4,000
5. Should children suffer for their fathers' sins?	**A.** Yes **B.** No
6. Judas died by	**A.** Bursting asunder **B.** Hanging himself
7. Has God ever been seen face to face?	**A.** Yes **B.** No
8. At the start of his reign, how old was Ahaziah?	**A.** 22 **B.** 42

See the answers on page 99.

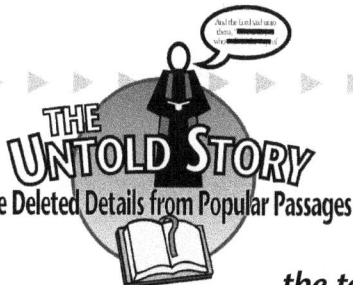

No longer do I call you servants, for the servant doesn't know what his lord does. But I have called you friends, for **everything that I heard from my Father, I have made known to you**.

John 15:15

——— & ———

I have still much to say to you, but you are not strong enough for it now.

John 16:12 ☙ *"Verily I say unto you, 'You can't handle the truth!'"*

THE UNTOLD STORY
The Deleted Details from Popular Passages

Now **this man purchased a field with the reward** of iniquity, and falling headlong, he burst asunder in the midst, and all his bowels gushed out.

Acts 1:18

——— & ———

And **he cast down the pieces of silver in the temple** and departed, and he went and hanged himself.

Matthew 27:5 ☙ *These authors disliked Judas so much, they killed him twice! Either way, it looks like Judas should have been under suicide watch.*

That Christ should suffer, and that he should be **the first that should rise from the dead**, and should show light to the people and to the Gentiles.
Acts 26:23

—— & ——

And when Elisha was come into the house, behold, the child was dead, and laid upon his bed. He went in therefore and shut the door upon them twain, and prayed unto the Lord. And he went up, and lay upon the child, and put his mouth upon his mouth, and his eyes upon his eyes, and his hands upon his hands, and stretched himself upon the child, and the flesh of the child waxed warm. Then he returned, and walked in the house to and fro, and went up, and stretched himself upon him, and **the child sneezed seven times**.
2 Kings 4:32-35 📖 *Not only was Jesus not the first to rise from the dead, he raised others from the dead when he was alive. Did the author of Acts not read the gospels?*

But I commend to you Phoebe, **our sister, who is minister of the assembly** which is in Cenchrea.
Romans 16:1

—— & ——

Let women keep quiet in the churches, for it is not right for them to be talking, but let them be under control, as it says in the law.
1 Corinthians 14:34 📖 *WWPS: What Would Phoebe Say?*

If any man among you seemeth to be wise in this world, let him **become a fool**, that he may be wise.
1 Corinthians 3:18

—— & ——

See then that ye walk circumspectly, **not as fools**, but as wise.
Ephesians 5:15 📖 *It's tough enough to try to not look like a fool, but to have to not be a fool while simultaneously being a fool, you would have to be pretty wise to figure that one out. Or maybe you'd be a fool to try.*

UNLIKELY SIGN
From a Fan in the Stands
1 Corinthians 12:31 — Covet gifts

But **covet earnestly the best gifts**. And yet I show to you a more excellent way.
1 Corinthians 12:31

—— & ——

For the commandments, "You shall not commit adultery," "You shall not murder," "You shall not steal," "You shall not give false testimony," "**You shall not covet**," and whatever other commandments there are, are all summed up in this saying, namely, "You shall love your neighbor as yourself."
Romans 13:9 📖 *You really shouldn't covet, but if you feel you absolutely have to covet something, you may as well covet the best gifts.*

Knowing that a man is not justified by the works of the law, but by the faith of Jesus Christ, even we have believed in Jesus Christ, that we might be justified by the faith of Christ, and not by the works of the law. For **by the works of the law shall no flesh be justified**.
Galatians 2:16
——— & ———
What does it profit, my brethren, if someone says he has faith but does not have works? **Can faith save him?**
James 2:14 🕮 *Let's flip a coin and decide this issue once and for all.*

Bear ye one another's burdens, and so fulfill the law of Christ.
Galatians 6:2
——— & ———
For each man shall **bear his own burden**.
Galatians 6:5 🕮 *The best Bible contradictions are the ones that are separated by only a few sentences.*

And for this cause, **God will give them up to the power of deceit** and they will put their faith in what is false.
2 Thessalonians 2:11
——— & ———
Lying lips are an abomination to Jehovah, but they that deal truly are his delight.
Proverbs 12:22 🕮 *Can you be anti-lying and pro-deceit at the same time? I guess some highly illogical things really are possible when you're the Almighty.*

I desire therefore that the men **pray in every place**, lifting up holy hands, without wrath and disputing.
1 Timothy 2:8
——— & ———
But when you make your prayer, **go into your private room**, and, shutting the door, say a prayer to your Father in secret, and your Father, who sees in secret, will give you your reward.
Matthew 6:6 🕮 *Of course, if you bring your private room with you every place you go, then you're covered.*

Bible Funmentionables'
EASIEST MULTIPLE CHOICE TEST ANSWERS

🕮 **If you've been paying attention, you most likely know that both A and B are true for all questions on p.97.**

1. The Lord is a man of war. –*Exod. 15:3*
   May the God of peace be with you all. –*Rom. 15:33*

2. Jacob begat Joseph. –*Matt. 1:16*
   Joseph, who was the son of Heli. –*Luke 3:23*

3. He is faithful…to cleanse us from all unrighteousness. –*1 John 1:9*
   Blaspheming against the Holy Spirit has no forgiveness. –*Mark 3:29*

4. Solomon had 40,000 stalls of horses for his chariots. –*1 Kings 4:26*
   Solomon had 4,000 stalls for horses and chariots. –*2 Chron. 9:25*

5. Prepare slaughter for his children for the iniquity of their fathers. –*Isa. 14:21*
   Neither shall the children be put to death for the fathers. –*Deut 24:16*

6. Judas burst asunder in the midst, and all his bowels gushed out. –*Acts 1:18*
   Judas hanged himself. –*Matt. 27:5*

7. For I have seen God face to face. –*Gen. 32:30*
   No man hath seen God at any time. –*John 1:18*

8. Twenty-two years old was Ahaziah when he began to reign. –*2 Kings 8:26*
   Forty-two years old was Ahaziah when he began to reign. –*2 Chron. 22:2*

For **the love of money is the root of all evil**, which some having aspired after, have wandered from the faith and pierced themselves with many sorrows.

1 Timothy 6:10

—— & ——

A feast is made for laughter, and wine makes the life glad. **Money is the answer for all things**.

Ecclesiastes 10:19 🜨 *Some disgraced preachers bring both of these passages to life by thinking money is the answer, but finding that they have pierced themselves with many sorrows, i.e. jail time.*

For this Melchizedek, the king of Salem, a priest of the Most High God, who gave Abraham his blessing, meeting him when he came back after putting the kings to death, and to whom Abraham gave a tenth part of everything which he had, being first named King of righteousness, and then in addition, King of Salem, that is to say, King of peace. **Being without father or mother, or family, having no birth or end to his life**, being made like the Son of God, is a priest forever.

Hebrews 7:1-3

—— & ——

And the man gave his wife the name of Eve because she was the mother of **all who have life**.

Genesis 3:20 🜨 *Melchizedek had no mother or father. Here's one genealogy that can't get messed up.*

Marriage is honorable in all, and the bed undefiled, but **whoremongers and adulterers God will judge**.

Hebrews 13:4

UNSAFE PASSAGE

Unsuitable for Student-Led Prayer

—— & ——

And the Lord said to Hosea, "Go, **take unto thee a wife of whoredoms** and children of whoredoms, for the land hath committed great whoredom, departing from the Lord."

Hosea 1:2 🜨 *For smiting, pestilence, and plagues, God is your go-to guy. Matchmaking? Not so much.*

𝒟o not give to a foolish man a foolish answer, or you will be like him.

Give to a foolish man a foolish answer, or he will seem wise to himself.

There is one lawgiver, who is able to save and to destroy. **Who art thou that judgest another?**
James 4:12

——— & ———

Ye shall do no unrighteousness in judgment. Thou shalt not respect the person of the poor, nor honor the person of the mighty, but **in righteousness shalt thou judge thy neighbor**.
Leviticus 19:15 🕮 *These two verses are both pretty persuasive. You judge for yourself.*

The heavens shall pass away with a great noise, and the elements shall melt with fervent heat. **The earth also and the works that are therein shall be burned up**.
2 Peter 3:10

——— & ———

One generation passeth away, and another generation cometh, but **the earth abideth forever**.
Ecclesiastes 1:4 🕮 *As the Bible's readers are apparently all earthlings, some clarity on this issue would put some minds at ease.*

He that loveth not knoweth not God, for **God is love**.
1 John 4:8

——— & ———

You shall not bow down yourself to them, nor serve them, for **I the Lord your God am a jealous God**, visiting the iniquity of the fathers on the children to the third and fourth generation of them that hate me.
Exodus 20:5

——— & ———

Love is patient and kind. **Love has no envy**. Love doesn't brag. Love has no pride.
1 Corinthians 13:4 🕮 *Either God just proved he doesn't exist, or he just put these verses in to see if we were paying attention.*

And I saw **a new heaven and a new earth**, for the first heaven and the first earth were gone, and there was no more sea.
Revelation 21:1

——— & ———

That which hath been is that which shall be, and that which hath been done is that which will be done. And **there is nothing new under the sun**.
Ecclesiastes 1:9 🕮 *There appears to be nothing new under the sea as well, because there appears to be no new sea.*

ODDS AND ENDS

FROM A TO Z

Some peculiarities in the Bible don't deserve lengthy examinations but are at least worthy of a quick mention. First in the list are the words you may not know (or be able to pronounce) followed by the more common words used in surprising ways. Unlike the previous chapters, many of the verses below have been shortened for the sake of brevity, clarity, and comedy.

A is for **Abijam** slept with his fathers. *1 Kings 15:8*

She said, "Let **Abishag** the Shunammite be given." *1 Kings 2:21*

Practices **abstemiousness** in all directions. *1 Corinthians 9:25*

Abiezer the **Anathothite**, Mebunnai the Hushathite. *2 Samuel 23:27*

The great and noble **Asnapper** brought over. *Ezra 4:10*

And the filth of the **afterbirths**, that come forth from between her feet, and the children that are born the same hour. For they shall eat them secretly. *Deuteronomy 28:57*

There were not found who did turn back to give glory to God, except this **alien**. *Luke 17:18*

With an anathema we did **anathematize** ourselves. *Acts 23:14*

Man did eat **angels**' food. *Psalms 78:25*

Go to the **ant**, O slothful one. *Proverbs 6:6*

The **ants** are not a strong people. *Proverbs 30:25*

They knew that they were naked. They sewed fig leaves together and made themselves **aprons**. *Genesis 3:7*

Thus saith the Lord God, "Woe to the women that sew pillows to all **armholes**." *Ezekiel 13:18*

Micah the Morashtite, who was a prophet in the days of Hezekiah, king of Judah, said to all the people of Judah, "This is what the Lord of **armies** has said." *Jeremiah 26:18*

Let the nations **arouse** themselves. *Joel 3:12*

And they went through the region of Phrygia and Galatia, having been forbidden of the Holy Spirit to speak the word in **Asia**. *Acts 16:6*

Thine **ass** shall be violently taken away from before thy face. *Deuteronomy 28:31*

And went **a-whoring** in their doings. *Psalms 106:39*

Should an **axe** brag against him who chops with it? Should a saw exalt itself above him who saws with it? As if a rod should lift those who lift it up, or as if a staff should lift up someone who is not wood. *Isaiah 10:15*

B is for **Baalath-beer-ramah** to the south. *Joshua 19:8*

And **Bakbakkar**, Heresh, and Galal. *1 Chronicles 9:15*

The children of **Bakbuk**, the children of Hakupha. *Ezra 2:51*

Dibon, and **Bamothbaal**, and Bethbaalmeon. *Joshua 13:17*

He surnamed them **Boanerges**. *Mark 3:17*

The children of Israel turned again and played the prostitute after the **Baals**. *Judges 8:33*

I shoe thee with **badger's** skin. *Ezekiel 16:10*

There came a lion and a **bear**, and took a lamb out of the flock. And I went out after him, and smote him, and delivered it out of his mouth. And when he arose against me, I caught him by his **beard** and smote him. *1 Samuel 17:34-35*

Jotham ran away, and fled, and went to **Beer**. *Judges 9:21*

Remembering thy breasts more than wine, the righteous love thee. I am **black** but beautiful. *Song of Songs 1:4-5*

With the **blast** of your nostrils, the waters were piled up. *Exodus 15:8*

The dogs licked up his **blood** where the prostitutes washed themselves, according to the word of Yahweh. *1 Kings 22:38*

But now God has put every one of the parts in the body as it was pleasing to him. And if they were all one part, where would the **body** be? *1 Corinthians 12:18-19*

HIDDEN BIBLE **BAND NAMES 1**

📖 When your rock band is about to hit the big time, it's important to have a great name all picked out. What better place to turn for inspiration than the book that's been a rock for so many. Below are just some of the possible band names taken straight from the Bible.

All These Utensils –*Exodus 25:39*

Angels of Evil –*Psalms 78:49*

Arrowsnake –*Isaiah 34:15*

Ashpenaz –*Daniel 1:3*

Axletrees –*1 Kings 7:33*

Band of Wrongdoers –*Psalms 26:5*

Beasts of the Wasteland –*Malachi 1:3*

Bow at Random –*1 Kings 22:34*

Bowels of Mercy –*Luke 1:78*

Cankerworm –*Nahum 3:15*

Centurion of the Band –*Acts 10:1*

Cometh Thither –*John 18:3*

Counsel of the Lads –*2 Chronicles 10:14*

Court for Owls –*Isaiah 34:13*

Craunch the Shards –*Ezekiel 23:34*

Cucumber-Garden –*Isaiah 1:8*

Thou shalt be for **booties** unto them? *Habakkuk 2:7*

And Salmon begat **Booz**, and Booz begat Obed. *Matthew 1:5*

And there was one of his disciples reclining in the **bosom** of Jesus, whom Jesus was loving. *John 13:23*

How greatly I long after you all in the **bowels** of Jesus Christ. *Philippians 1:8*

Ten women shall bake your **bread** in one oven. *Leviticus 26:26*

You shall make them linen **breeches** to cover the flesh of their nakedness. They shall be on Aaron and his sons when they go in to the Tent of Meeting, that they don't bear iniquity and die. *Exodus 28:42-43*

If you come across the dead body of a man in the open country, and you have no idea who has put him to death, then whichever town is nearest the body, the responsible men of that town are to take from the herd a young cow into a valley where there is flowing water, and there the neck of the cow is to be **broken**. And all the responsible men of that town, washing their hands over the cow will say, "This death is not the work of our hands." *Deuteronomy 21:1-4,6-7*

And they go a-whoring in Egypt. In their youth they have gone a-whoring. There they have **bruised** their breasts. *Ezekiel 23:3*

C is for *Chenaanah* came near and struck. *1 Kings 22:24*

Lahmas and **Chithlish**. *Joshua 15:40*

The hand of **Chushanrishathaim** king of Mesopotamia. *Judges 3:8*

Not in the lust of **concupiscence**, even as the Gentiles. *1 Thessalonians 4:5*

And the **captain** of the Lord's army said to Joshua, "Take off your shoes." *Joshua 5:15*

A **carbuncle**, this shall be the first row. *Exodus 28:17*

And all the mingled people and **Chub**.
Ezekiel 30:5

Drowsiness **clotheth** with rags.
Proverbs 23:21

I will seem disgusting to my very **clothing**.
Job 9:31

An Affiliate of the Rejoicing Ostrich Wing Church

NEW HOPE MILLENIUM

"THOU HAST LOVED HARLOT'S HIRE UPON EVERY CORN-FLOOR" HOSEA 9:1

Ye do not eat with the blood, ye do not enchant, nor observe **clouds**. *Leviticus 19:26*

And the sucking child shall play on the hole of the asp, and the weaned child shall put his hand on the **cockatrice**'s den. *Isaiah 11:8*

And he had a son whose name was Saul, choice and **comely**.
1 Samuel 9:2

And the Lord visited Hannah, so that she **conceived**. *1 Samuel 2:21*

Absalom went in unto his father's **concubines** in the sight of all Israel. *2 Samuel 16:22*

He is only relieving himself in the closet of the **cool chamber**. *Judges 3:24*

The woman also with whom man shall lie with seed of **copulation**, they shall both bathe themselves in water and be unclean until the evening. *Leviticus 15:18*

Let the king appoint officers in all the provinces of his kingdom, that they may gather together all the beautiful young virgins to the citadel of Susa, to the women's house, to the custody of Hegai the king's eunuch, keeper of the women. Let **cosmetics** be given them. *Esther 2:3*

And take with thee ten loaves, and **cracknels**, and a cruse of honey. *1 Kings 14:3*

Then said his wife unto him, "Dost thou still retain thine integrity? **Curse** God, and die." *Job 2:9*

And these ten **cuttings** of the cheese thou dost take in to the head of the thousand. *1 Samuel 17:18*

D is for *Dibongad*. *Numbers 33:45*

Then Eliezer the son of **Dodavahu**. *2 Chronicles 20:37*

There was a certain **dropsical** man before him. *Luke 14:2*

And turning to her by the roadside, he said to her, "Let me come in to you," for he had no idea that she was his **daughter-in-law**. And she said, "What will you give me as my price?" *Genesis 38:16*

▶ I will not punish your **daughters** when they commit whoredom. *Hosea 4:14*

Don't be desirous of his **dainties**, seeing they are deceitful food. *Proverbs 23:3*

HIDDEN BIBLE
BAND NAMES 2

🎵 Coming up with a good name has been important for millennia, as can be seen in this verse: "I named Bands, and I fed the flock." – *Zechariah 11:7*

Dainty Meat –*Job 33:20*

Dead Corpses –*Isaiah 37:36*

Death Blow, Because –*2 Samuel 1:10*

Deceptive Food –*Proverbs 23:3*

Demetrius and the Mechanics –*Acts 19:38*

Dog-Fly –*Psalms 105:31*

Dust of the Burned Cow –*Numbers 19:10*

Family of the Oznites –*Numbers 26:16*

Feast-Master –*John 2:8*

Fellowship of the Demons –*1 Corinthians 10:20*

Flog a Scoffer –*Proverbs 19:25*

Flock of Jethro –*Exodus 3:1*

Frogs the Nile –*Exodus 8:2-3*

Agag cometh unto him **daintily**. *1 Samuel 15:32*

So that his life abhorreth bread, and his soul **dainty** meat. *Job 33:20*

My rock, don't be **deaf** to me. *Psalms 28:1*

And the kings of the earth, who have committed fornication and lived **deliciously** with her, shall bewail her and lament for her, when they shall see the smoke of her burning. *Revelation 18:9*

The **destroyers** have destroyed them. *Nahum 2:2*

The dragon stood before the woman who was about to give birth, so that when she gave birth he might **devour** her child. *Revelation 12:4*

UNLIKELY SIGN
From a Fan in the Stands

Matthew 23:23

Don't tithe dill

▶ "Woe to you, scribes and Pharisees, hypocrites! For you tithe mint, **dill**, and cumin." *Matthew 23:23*

No **disgusting** thing may be your food. *Deuteronomy 14:3*

Thou shalt not bring the hire of a whore or the price of a **dog**. *Deuteronomy 23:18*

No **dog-flies** shall be there, that thou mayest know that I Jehovah am in the midst of the land. *Exodus 8:22*

Am I a **dog's head** that belongs to Judah? *2 Samuel 3:8*

And Elisha said, "I pray thee, let a **double** portion of thy spirit be upon me." *2 Kings 2:9*

I am a brother to **dragons** and a companion to owls. *Job 30:29*

And Jehovah said to Moses, "Take fragrant **drugs**, stacte, and onycha, and galbanum, fragrant drugs and pure frankincense." *Exodus 30:34*

The **dumb** ass speaking with man's voice forbad the madness of the prophet. *2 Peter 2:16*

Behold, I will corrupt your seed, and spread **dung** upon your faces, even the dung of your solemn feasts. *Malachi 2:3*

The way of the Lord is in the wind and the storm, and the clouds are the **dust** of his feet. *Nahum 1:3*

E is for *Ephesdammim*. *1 Samuel 17:1*

In Damascus the **ethnarc** of King Aretas kept the city. *2 Corinthians 11:32*

I exhort **Euodia**, and I exhort Syntyche. *Philippians 4:2*

That **Evilmerodach** king of Babylon. *2 Kings 25:27*

Let the hair be pulled from your head like an **eagle's**. *Micah 1:16*

They shall take away thy nose and thine **ears**. *Ezekiel 23:25*

Is there any taste in the white of an **egg**? *Job 6:6*

They that were brought up in scarlet **embrace** dunghills. *Lamentations 4:5*

And Esau runneth to meet him, and **embraceth** him, and falleth on his neck. *Genesis 33:4*

Eat not of it raw, nor boiled at all with water, but roasted with fire; its head with its legs, and with its **entrails**. *Exodus 12:9*

I found also an **erection** on which had been inscribed: "To the God of whom there is no knowledge." *Acts 17:23*

And if one person sin through **error**, then he shall offer a she-goat of the first year for a sin-offering. *Numbers 15:27*

UNSAFE PASSAGE
Unsuitable for Student-Led Prayer

"Why, how can I," replied the **eunuch**, "unless some one explains it to me?" *Acts 8:31*

Thou shalt not sacrifice unto the Lord thy God any bullock, or sheep, wherein is blemish, or any **evilfavouredness**. *Deuteronomy 17:1*

My wounds are poisoned and **evil-smelling**. *Psalms 38:5*

Whether it is a cow or **ewe**, you shall not kill it and its young both in one day. *Leviticus 22:28*

The **eye** that mocks at his father and scorns obedience to his mother, the ravens of the valley shall pick it out. The young eagles shall eat it. *Proverbs 30:17*

Their **eyes** are bursting with fat. *Psalms 73:7*

F is for *fellow-feeling*, loving as brethren. *1 Peter 3:8*

Change it into fifty **firkins**. *Luke 16:6*

A cry from the **fish-gate** and a howling. *Zephaniah 1:10*

Of great kindness, and **forsookest** them not. *Nehemiah 9:17*

PITY THE TRANSLATOR 6

You may have never felt the urge to eat a ferret or any of the other "creeping things that creep," but just to make it official, Leviticus 11:30 informs us of the specific creatures that are on the unclean list.

" And the **ferret**, and the **chameleon**, and the **lizard**, and the **snail**, and the **mole**.

Ferret
King James

gecko
American Standard Version

shrew
Douay-Rheims Bible

groaning lizard
Darby Bible Translation

Chameleon
King James

land-crocodile
American Standard Version

great red lizard
Darby Bible Translation

monitor lizard
World English Bible

Lizard
King James

stellio
Douay-Rheims Bible

climbing lizard
Darby Bible Translation

wall lizard
World English Bible

Snail
King James

sand-lizard
American Standard Version

lizard
Douay-Rheims Bible

chomet
Darby Bible Translation

skink
World English Bible

Mole
King James

chameleon
American Standard Version

Saith Jehovah, "I have been satiated with burnt-offerings of rams and **fat of fatlings**." *Isaiah 1:11*

Giving no attention to the **fictions** of the Jews. *Titus 1:14*

The stars from heaven were **fighting**. From their highways they were fighting against Sisera. *Judges 5:20*

He who acts unjustly, let him act unjustly still. He who is **filthy**, let him be filthy still. *Revelation 22:11*

Their **fish** stink, because there is no water, and die for thirst. *Isaiah 50:2*

The head of Dagon and both the palms of his hands were cut off upon the threshold. Only the **fish-stump** was left to him. *1 Samuel 5:4*

My knees are weak through fasting and my **flesh faileth of fatness**. *Psalms 109:24*

If any man lie with a woman in her **flowers** and uncover her nakedness, and she open the fountain of her blood, both shall be destroyed out of the midst of their people. *Leviticus 20:18*

Speak unto the children of Israel, and say unto them, "If any man have a **flux from** his **flesh**, because of his flux he is unclean." *Leviticus 15:2*

Two wings of the great eagle were given to the woman, that she might **fly** into the wilderness. *Revelation 12:14*

Every prudent man worketh with knowledge, but a **fool flaunteth folly**. *Proverbs 13:16*

Drink thou also, and let thy **foreskin** be uncovered. *Habakkuk 2:16*

The **frogs** came up and covered the land of Egypt. And the magicians did so with their enchantments and brought up frogs. *Exodus 8:6-7*

G is for **Gadgad**, from which place they departed. *Deuteronomy 10:7*

Called in my hearing, **Galgal**. *Ezekiel 10:13*

And its villages, and **Gimzo** and its villages. *2 Chronicles 28:18*

Daniel, **Ginnethon**. *Nehemiah 10:6*

On the east to **Gittahhepher**. *Joshua 19:13*

That also was accounted a land of **giants**. Giants dwelt therein in old time, and the Ammonites call them Zamzummims. *Deuteronomy 2:20*

And for Aaron's sons thou shalt make coats, and thou shalt make for them **girdles**, and bonnets shalt thou make for them, for glory and for beauty. *Exodus 28:40*

There are three things, the wonder of which overcomes me, even four things outside my knowledge: the way of an eagle in the air, the way of a snake on a rock, the way of a ship in the heart of the sea, and the way of a man with a **girl**. *Proverbs 30:18-19*

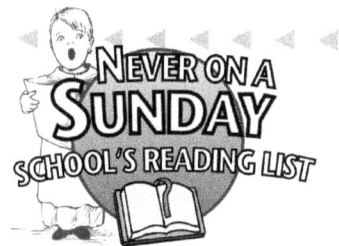

The spirit of **God** is in my nostrils. *Job 27:3*

He shall exalt himself, and magnify himself above every god, and shall speak marvellous things against the God of **gods**. *Daniel 11:36*

"The silver is mine, and the **gold** is mine," saith the Lord of hosts. *Haggai 2:8*

And David letteth down the **goods**. *1 Samuel 17:22*

So Jonah was exceeding glad of the **gourd**. *Jonah 4:6*

The Lord knoweth how to reserve the unjust unto the day of judgment to be punished. But chiefly them that walk after the flesh in the lust of uncleanness and despise **government**. *2 Peter 2:9-10*

Drink the pure blood of the **grape**. *Deuteronomy 32:14*

And the Lord said to me, "Give your love again to a woman who has a lover and is false to her husband, even as the Lord has love for the children of Israel, though they are turned to other gods and are lovers of **grape-cakes**." *Hosea 3:1*

Canst thou make him afraid as a **grasshopper**? *Job 39:20*

And there we saw the giants, the sons of Anak, which come of the giants, and we were in our own sight as **grasshoppers**. *Numbers 13:33*

I have a debt to **Greeks**. *Romans 1:14*

For of these are those who creep into houses and take captive **gullible** women loaded down with sins, led away by various lusts. *2 Timothy 3:6*

H is for *Hadadezer* at their head. *1 Chronicles 19:16*

A homer of barley and a **half-homer** of barley. *Hosea 3:2*

Hashum and **Hashbadana**. *Nehemiah 8:4*

Haroeh, **Hazi-Hammenuhoth**. *1 Chronicles 2:52*

How **holily** and justly and unblameably. *1 Thessalonians 2:10*

They shall be **holpen** with a little help. *Daniel 11:34*

And they went from **Horhagidgad** and pitched in Jotbathah. *Numbers 33:33*

Huz his firstborn and Buz his brother. *Genesis 22:21*

So there was **hail** and fire mingled with the hail. *Exodus 9:24*

Till his **hairs** were grown like eagles' feathers and his nails like birds' claws. *Daniel 4:33*

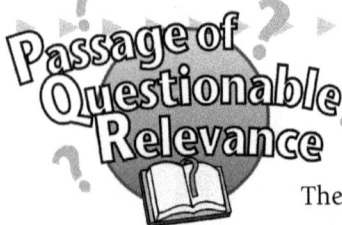

Passage of Questionable Relevance

And you, son of man, take a sharp sword, using it like a **haircutter's** blade, and making it go over your head and the hair of your chin, and take scales for separating the hair by weight. *Ezekiel 5:1*

The firstborn came out red all over, like a **hairy** garment. *Genesis 25:25*

Will you **harass** a driven leaf? *Job 13:25*

There hath been no latter rain, yet thou hast a **harlot's** forehead. *Jeremiah 3:3*

Wherefore my bowels shall sound like a **harp**. *Isaiah 16:11*

If two lie together, then they have **heat**. *Ecclesiastes 4:11*

And the king of Egypt speaketh to the midwives, the **Hebrewesses**. *Exodus 1:15*

And I will make you a heritage for the **hedgehog** and pools of water. *Isaiah 14:23*

Egypt is a very fair **heifer**. The gad-fly cometh. *Jeremiah 46:20*

And the men that died not were smitten with the **hemorrhoids**. *1 Samuel 5:12*

And the Lord answered, "Behold he hath **hid** himself among the stuff." *1 Samuel 10:22*

Joshua made himself flint knives and circumcised the children of Israel at the **hill** of the foreskins. *Joshua 5:3*

The Lord hath made all things for **himself**. Yea, even the wicked for the day of evil. *Proverbs 16:4*

Then after that he saith to his disciples, "Let us **ho** into Judea again." *John 11:7*

And even to **hoar hairs** will I carry you. *Isaiah 46:4*

For in their anger they slew a man, and in their self-will they **hocked** an ox. *Genesis 49:6*

Which say, "Stand by thyself, come not near to me, for I am **holier** than thou. These are a smoke in my nose." *Isaiah 65:5*

For ten acres of vineyard shall yield one bath and a **homer**. *Isaiah 5:10*

Therefore will I put my **hook** in your nose. *2 Kings 19:28*

But my **horn** shalt thou exalt like the horn of a unicorn. *Psalms 92:10*

And I sent the **hornet** before you, driving out the two kings of the Amorites before you. *Joshua 24:12*

God had **horns** coming out of his hand. *Habakkuk 3:4*

Unlike most teachers, we are not fraudulent **hucksters** of God's message. *2 Corinthians 2:17*

Every man **hunts** his brother with a net. *Micah 7:2*

I

I is for *Idbash* and their sister's name was Hazzelelponi. *1 Chronicles 4:3*

Hath found the *Imim* in the wilderness. *Genesis 36:24*

Who hath the scribe's *inkhorn* at his loins. *Ezekiel 9:4*

Puvah, *Iob*, and Shimron. *Genesis 46:13*

And *Ishbibenob*, who was of the sons of the giant. *2 Samuel 21:16*

They took the head of *Ishbosheth* and buried it in the grave of Abner. *2 Samuel 4:12*

The head *Ishshiah*. *1 Chronicles 24:21*

Out of whose womb came the *ice*? *Job 38:29*

I will send down on him great *ice-drops*, fire, and burning. *Ezekiel 38:22*

As they looked on Peter and John so fearlessly outspoken, and also discovered that they were *illiterate* persons. *Acts 4:13*

For my loins are filled with *illusions*. *Psalms 38:7*

And ye shall make *images* of your hemorrhoids and images of your mice. *1 Samuel 6:5*

For if that first covenant had been free from *imperfection*, there would have been no attempt to introduce another. *Hebrews 8:7*

That Satan may not tempt you for your *incontinence*. *1 Corinthians 7:5*

The priest shall pronounce him clean, for it is an *inflammation* of the burning. *Leviticus 13:28*

"Paul, you are crazy! Your great learning is driving you *insane*!" *Acts 26:24*

My kidneys also *instruct* me in the nights. *Psalms 16:7*

We who held sweet *intercourse* together, to the house of God we walked amid the throng. *Psalms 55:14*

For this is not *intoxication*, as you suppose, it being only the third hour of the day. *Acts 2:15*

Seeing him who is *invisible*. *Hebrews 11:27*

Can you fill his skin with barbed *irons* or his head with fish spears? *Job 41:7*

They of *Italy* salute you. *Hebrews 13:24*

J is for *Jaareoregim* the Bethlehemite killed Goliath. *2 Samuel 21:19*

Of ***Jeduthun***, the sons of Jeduthun. *1 Chronicles 25:3*

Chief Aliah, Chief ***Jetheth***. *1 Chronicles 1:51*

Amram took ***Jochebed*** his father's sister as wife. *Exodus 6:20*

For ***Jozacar*** the son of Shimeath. *2 Kings 12:21*

I will go stripped and naked. I will howl like the ***jackals*** and moan like the daughters of owls. *Micah 1:8*

Therefore the children of Israel don't eat the sinew of the hip, which is on the hollow of the thigh, to this day, because he touched the hollow of ***Jacob***'s thigh in the sinew of the hip. *Genesis 32:32*

And the evil spirit from the Lord was upon Saul, as he sat in his house with his ***javelin*** in his hand, and David played with his hand. *1 Samuel 19:9*

But the man would not tarry that night, but he arose and departed, and came over against ***Jebus***. *Judges 19:10*

The just, the blameless man is a ***joke***. *Job 12:4*

All countries came into Egypt to ***Joseph*** for to buy corn. *Genesis 41:57*

And ***Joshua*** fell on his face. *Joshua 5:14*

But wicked men and ***juggling*** impostors shall advance in evil. *2 Timothy 3:13*

Neither shall he drink any ***juice*** of grapes, nor eat fresh grapes or dried. *Numbers 6:3*

HIDDEN BIBLE **BAND NAMES 3**

Music is an important part of many religious services. Jesus did say "upon this rock I will build my church" in Matthew 16:18. Though it is widely believed he never uttered the phrase, "A band is only as cool as its name."

Garments of Vengeance –*Isaiah 59:17*	**It Were Frogs** –*Revelation 16:13*	**Mind Deceivers** –*Titus 1:10*
A Great Band (with swords) –*Mark 14:43*	**Kick Against the Pricks** –*Acts 9:5*	**Mingled Motives** –*1 Thessalonians 2:3*
Heathen Rage –*Acts 4:25*	**Kings of the Land of the Uz** –*Jeremiah 25:20*	
The House of an Alien –*Proverbs 5:10*		**No Small Disturbance** –*Acts 19:23*
Howl for the Grape-Cakes –*Isaiah 16:7*	**Land of Death-Shade** –*Isaiah 9:2*	
	Master of His Eunuchs –*Daniel 1:3*	**Noise of an Uproar** –*Isaiah 13:4*

K is for Kaiwan your images, the star of your god. *Amos 5:26*

The name of that place **Kibrothhattaavah**, for there are buried lusters. *Numbers 11:34*

Butter of **kine** and milk of sheep. *Deuteronomy 32:14*

And they came unto **Kirjathhuzoth**. *Numbers 22:39*

Your **kerchiefs** also will I tear, and ye shall know that I am the Lord. *Ezekiel 13:21*

And he struck it into the pan, or **kettle**, or cauldron. *1 Samuel 2:14*

His archers surround me. He splits my **kidneys** apart. *Job 16:13*

Submit yourselves to every ordinance of man for the Lord's sake, whether it be to the **king**, as supreme or unto governors. *1 Peter 2:13-14*

And he cometh nigh, and **kisseth** him, and he smelleth the fragrance of his garments. *Genesis 27:27*

PITY THE TRANSLATOR 7

You're lost in the forest searching for food, and you see a locust—what do you do? Leviticus 11:22 says it's lunchtime! But wait. Are you sure that's not a bruchus or an arbeh?

Even these of them ye may eat: the **locust** after his kind, and the **bald locust** after his kind, and the **beetle** after his kind, and the **grasshopper** after his kind.

Locust
King James

bruchus
Douay-Rheims Bible

arbeh
Darby Bible Translation

Bald locust
King James

attacus
Douay-Rheims Bible

solum
Darby Bible Translation

katydid
World English Bible

Beetle
King James

cricket
American Standard Version

ophiomachus
Douay-Rheims Bible

hargol
Darby Bible Translation

Grasshopper
King James

locust
Douay-Rheims Bible

hargab
Darby Bible Translation

And he said to me, "This is the house of the **kitchens** wherein the ministers of the house of the Lord shall boil the victims of the people." *Ezekiel 46:24*

Their **kneadingtroughs** being bound up in their clothes upon their shoulders. *Exodus 12:34*

And Cain **knew** his wife, and she conceived. *Genesis 4:17*
And Joseph **knew** his brethren, but they knew not him. *Genesis 42:8*

And crouched in her midst have droves, every beast of the nation, both pelican and hedgehog in her **knobs** lodge. *Zephaniah 2:14*

And a **knop** under two branches of the same, and a **knop** under two branches of the same, and a **knop** under two branches of the same, according to the six branches going out of it. *Exodus 37:21*

Knotting his ass's cord to the vine and his young ass to the best vine. *Genesis 49:11*

L is for *ladeth* himself with thick clay. *Habakkuk 2:6*

No one buys their *lading* any more. *Revelation 18:11*

He said to Simon, "*Lanch* out into the deep." *Luke 5:4*

Not in chamberings and *lasciviousnesses*, not in strife and emulation. *Romans 13:13*

And their sins and their *lawlessnesses* I will never remember any more. *Hebrews 8:12*

But ye have not thus *learnt* the Christ. *Ephesians 4:20*

In Tyrannus's *lecture-hall*. *Acts 19:9*

Only he who now *letteth* will let. *2 Thessalonians 2:7*

Ethiopia, and Put, and *Lud*, and all the mixed people, and Cub. *Ezekiel 30:5*

Have they not divided the spoil? A lady, two *ladies* to every man? *Judges 5:30*

Jesus, therefore, saith to them, "*Lads*, have ye any meat?" *John 21:5*

And the Lord said to Gideon, "Every one that *laps* the water with his tongue, as a dog laps, you shall set by himself. *Judges 7:5*

A feast of fat things, a feast of wines on the *lees*. *Isaiah 25:6*

Like the *legs* of the *lame* that hang *loose*, so is a parable in the mouth of fools. *Proverbs 26:7*

The inhabitants of the earth have been made drunk with the wine of her *lewdness*. *Revelation 17:2*

The magicians tried with their enchantments to bring forth *lice*. *Exodus 8:18*

They will *lick* the dust like a serpent. *Micah 7:17*

As the ox *licketh* up the grass of the field. *Numbers 22:4*

And when he shall go to sleep, mark the place wherein he sleepeth, and thou shalt go in, and *lift* up the clothes wherewith he is covered towards his feet, and shalt lay thyself down there, and he will tell thee what thou must do. *Ruth 3:4*

UNSAFE PASSAGE
Unsuitable for Student-Led Prayer

And it came to pass through the *lightness* of her whoredom, that she defiled the land and committed adultery with stones and with stocks. *Jeremiah 3:9*

Canst thou send **lightnings**, that they may go and say unto thee, "Here we are?" *Job 38:35*

Who makes the judges of the earth **like** meaningless. *Isaiah 40:23*

A living dog is better than a dead **lion**. *Ecclesiastes 9:4*

The lion tore in pieces enough for his cubs and strangled for his **lionesses**. *Nahum 2:12*

He slew two **lionlike** men of Moab. He went down also and slew a lion in the midst of a pit in time of snow. *2 Samuel 23:20*

Moses said before Yahweh, "Behold, I am of uncircumcised **lips**." *Exodus 6:30*

Thy navel is like a round goblet, which lacketh not **liquor**. Thy belly is like a heap of wheat set about with lilies. *Song of Songs 7:2*

Thou shalt not delay to offer the first of thy ripe fruits and of thy **liquors**. The firstborn of thy sons shalt thou give unto me. *Exodus 22:29*

And that there may not be any evil **liver**. *Hebrews 12:16*

Neither is there any water, and our soul **loatheth** this light bread. *Numbers 21:5*

If his **loins** have not blessed me. *Job 31:20*

He **looked** in the liver. *Ezekiel 21:21*

For the inhabitant of Maroth waited carefully for good, but evil came down from the **Lord**. *Micah 1:12*

These men are unseen rocks at your **love-feasts**. *Jude 1:12*

The fir trees rejoice with you saying, "Since you are humbled, no **lumberjack** has come up against us." *Isaiah 14:8*

If the first fruit is holy, so is the **lump**. *Romans 11:16*

Jesus said, "When you give a **luncheon** or a dinner, do not invite your friends or brothers or relatives." *Luke 14:12*

And they tempted God in their heart by asking meat for their **lust**. *Psalms 78:18*

And thou shalt bestow that money for whatsoever thy soul **lusteth** after, for oxen, or for sheep, or for wine, or for strong drink. *Deuteronomy 14:26*

M is for Madmannah and Sansannah. *Joshua 15:31*

Write with a man's pen **Mahershalalhashbaz**. *Isaiah 8:1*

The best and **meetest** of your master's sons. *2 Kings 10:3*

Yahweh that came to **Micah the Morashtite** in the days of Jotham. *Micah 1:1*

At **Michmash** he stores his baggage. *Isaiah 10:28*

They take to them wives **Moabitesses**, the name of the one is Orpah. *Ruth 1:4*

Give presents to **Moreshethgath**. *Micah 1:14*

He feigned himself **mad** in their hands, and scrabbled on the doors of the gate, and let his spittle fall down upon his beard. *1 Samuel 21:13*

Like a **madman** who shoots torches, arrows, and death. *Proverbs 26:18*

Yes, you would even cast lots for the fatherless and **make merchandise** of your friend. *Job 6:27*

And you took the fair jewels, my silver and gold which I had given to you, and made for yourself **male** images, acting like a loose woman with them. *Ezekiel 16:17*

Who cut up **mallows** by the bushes and juniper roots for their **meat**. *Job 30:4*

How much less **man**, that is a worm! And the son of man, that is a worm! *Job 25:6*

Speak unto the children of Israel, saying, "If a woman have conceived seed and born a **man-child**, then she shall be unclean seven days, but if she bear a **maid-child**, then she shall be unclean two weeks." *Leviticus 12:2,5*

Then the angel of the Lord put out the stick which was in his hand, touching the **meat** and the cakes with the end of it, and a flame came up out of the rock, burning up the meat and the cakes. *Judges 6:21*

But he answered and said, "It is not **meet** to take the children's bread and to cast it to dogs." *Matthew 15:26*

His bones are tubes of bronze. His **members** are like bars of iron. *Job 40:18*

I gat me **men-singers** and women-singers. *Ecclesiastes 2:8*

Thou shalt cast them away as a **menstruous** cloth. *Isaiah 30:22*

As newborn babes desire earnestly the pure **mental milk** of the word. *1 Peter 2:2*

If a man be found stealing any of his brethren of the children of Israel, and maketh **merchandise** of him, or selleth him, then that thief shall die. *Deuteronomy 24:7*

They called Barnabas "Jupiter," and Paul "**Mercury**." *Acts 14:12*

Can you, with him, spread out the sky, which is strong as a cast **metal mirror**? *Job 37:18*

Then they said, "What is the trespass-offering which we shall return to him?" And they said, "Five golden hemorrhoids and five golden **mice**." *1 Samuel 6:4*

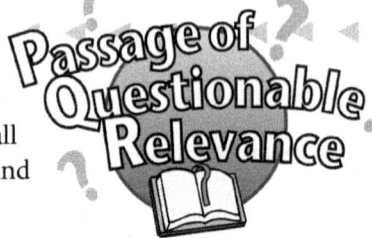

Therefore the building was straitened more than the lowest and the **middlemost** from the ground. *Ezekiel 42:6*

This is the law of the plague of **mildew**. *Leviticus 13:59*

Double unto her the double according to her works. In the cup which she **mingled**, **mingle** unto her double. *Revelation 18:6*

> Cursed are those who are strong to take wine and great in making **mixed** drinks! *Isaiah 5:22*

His pails are full of milk. The marrow of his bones is **moistened**. *Job 21:24*

In that day, men shall cast away their idols of silver, and their idols of gold, which have been made for themselves to worship, to the **moles** and to the bats. *Isaiah 2:20*

The sea **monsters** draw out the breast, they give suck to their young. *Lamentations 4:3*

A wild ass, accustomed to the wilderness in the desire of his heart, snuffed up the wind of his love. None shall turn her away. All that seek her shall not fail. In her **monthly** filth they shall find her. *Jeremiah 2:24*

The sun shall not burn thee by day, nor the **moon** by night. *Psalms 121:6*

> In that day, the Lord will take away the glory of their foot-rings, and their sun-jewels, and their **moon-ornaments**. *Isaiah 3:18*

He builds his house as the **moth**. *Job 27:18*

And the **mountains** have dropt juice. *Amos 9:13*

For thus said Jehovah "Do not enter the house of a **mourning-feast**." *Jeremiah 16:5*

Whoever hates his brother is a **murderer**. *1 John 3:15*

Would to God that those who are unsettling your faith would even **mutilate** themselves. *Galatians 5:12*

As a bag of **myrrh** is my well-loved one to me, when he is at rest all night between my breasts. *Song of Songs 1:13*

N is for Nebushazban, chief of the eunuchs. *Jeremiah 39:13*

By his **neesings** a light doth shine. *Job 41:18*

The porters and the **Nethinims** dwelt in their cities. *Ezra 2:70*

Wherefore lay apart all filthiness and superfluity of **naughtiness**. *James 1:21*

And his life hath **nauseated** bread, and his soul desirable food. *Job 33:20*

It shall be health to thy **navel**. *Proverbs 3:8*

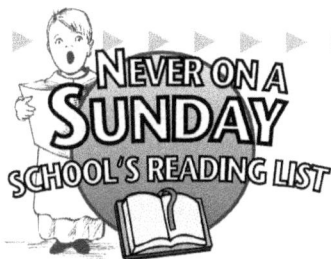

NEVER ON A SUNDAY SCHOOL'S READING LIST

They were as fed horses roaming at large. Everyone **neighed** after his **neighbor's** wife. *Jeremiah 5:8*

Purge out the old yeast, that you may be a **new** lump. *1 Corinthians 5:7*

Your **nose** is as the tower of Lebanon looking over Damascus. *Song of Songs 7:4*

And they put him in a cage with **nose-rings**. *Ezekiel 19:9*

If the whole body were an ear, where would the **nostrils** be? *1 Corinthians 12:17*

And Enoch walked with God, and he was **not**, for God took him. *Genesis 5:24*

As he says also in Hosea, "I will call **not-my-people** 'My People,' and the-not-beloved 'Beloved.'" *Romans 9:25*

There are many servants **now-a-days** that break away every man from his master. *1 Samuel 25:10*

To those others outside your **number** all this is spoken in figurative language, that they may look and look but not see, and listen and listen but not understand, lest perchance they should return and be pardoned. *Mark 4:11-12*

Carry them in thy bosom, as a **nursing-father** carrieth the sucking child. *Numbers 11:12*

O is for Obededom with joy. *1 Chronicles 15:25*

He sent for him the **oftener** and communed with him. *Acts 24:26*

Chief **Oholibamah**, chief Elah, chief Pinon. *Genesis 36:41*

It was as the taste of **oil-cakes**. *Numbers 11:8*

Two cherubs of the **oil-tree**, ten cubits is their height. *1 Kings 6:23*

Take a pot, and put an **omerful** of manna therein. *Exodus 16:33*

Together with **Onesimus**, the faithful and beloved brother. *Colossians 4:9*

The way that leads to **Ophrah**. *1 Samuel 13:17*

And thou shalt make **ouches** of gold. *Exodus 28:13*

HIDDEN BIBLE BAND NAMES 4

Careful (and highly selective) reading of the Bible can be encouraging to the up-and-coming band. Psalms 71:3 clearly states "...rock on..."!

Ointment of Spikenard *–Mark 14:3*

Pluck Off *–Ezekiel 23:34*

Possession of the Hedgehog *–Isaiah 14:23*

Rage Ye Peoples *–Isaiah 8:9*

Red Ass's Mouth-Bone *–Judges 15:16*

Rock of Offense *–1 Peter 2:8*

Rock My Fortress *–2 Samuel 22:2*

Seals Up the Hand *–Job 37:7*

Sick of the Palsy *–Mark 2:3*

Secrets of Satan *–Revelation 2:24*

A Seller of Purple *–Acts 16:14*

Sham Apostles *–2 Corinthians 11:13*

Smiters and I *–Psalms 35:15*

Smoking Against the Sheep *–Psalms74:1*

Smote the People *–Numbers 11:33*

Sons of Thunder *–Mark 3:17*

Stones of Emptiness *–Isaiah 34:11*

Suburbs for Our Livestock *–Joshua 21:2*

Who can **open** the doors of his face? *Job 41:14*

And Paul, having stood in the midst of the Areopagus, said, "Men, Athenians, in all things I perceive you as **over-religious**." *Acts 17:22*

And after him came Shamgar, the son of Anath, who put to death six hundred Philistines with an **ox-stick**. *Judges 3:31*

P is for paps with a golden girdle. *Revelation 1:13*

Beans, and lentils, and **parched pulse**. *2 Samuel 17:28*

He is in a journey, or **peradventure** he sleepeth. *1 Kings 18:27*

The family of the **Perezites**. *Numbers 26:20*

And he maketh the **perfume-altar** of shittim wood. *Exodus 37:25*

They make their broad **phylacteries**. *Matthew 23:5*

And Jehovah **plagueth** them that made the calf that Aaron made. *Exodus 32:35*

Lay a cake of figs for a **poultice** on the boil, and he shall recover. *Isaiah 38:21*

Ephraim is a **pancake** not turned over. *Hosea 7:8*

The unsexed servants and the priests and all the people of the land who went between the **parts** of the ox. *Jeremiah 34:19*

He withdrew and separated himself for fear of the circumcision **party**. *Galatians 2:12*

Or hath his **peculiar** members broken. *Leviticus 21:20*

I hate them with **perfect** hatred. I count them mine enemies. *Psalms 139:22*

Then fire came out from the Lord, burning up the two hundred and fifty men who were offering the **perfume**. *Numbers 16:35*

Yet he shall **perish** forever like his own dung. They which have seen him shall say, "Where is he?" *Job 20:7*

You are not to make an image or **picture** of anything in heaven, or on the earth, or in the waters under the earth. *Exodus 20:4*

Thus saith the Lord God, "Behold, I am against your **pillows**." *Ezekiel 13:20*

The adversary hath spread out his hand upon all her **pleasant** things, for she hath seen that the heathen entered into her sanctuary. *Lamentations 1:10*

If possible, you would have **plucked** out your eyes and given them to me. *Galatians 4:15*

On its hem you shall make **pomegranates** of blue. *Exodus 28:33*

Both the pelican and the **porcupine** shall lodge in the capitals thereof. Their voice shall sing in the windows. *Zephaniah 2:14*

Woe to those who are **pregnant** and those who nurse infants in those days! *Luke 21:23*

But God **prepared** a worm at dawn the next day. *Jonah 4:7*

It is hard for thee to kick against the **pricks**. *Acts 26:14*

For bodily exercise **profiteth** little. *1 Timothy 4:8*

Now Philip had four unmarried daughters who were **prophetesses**. *Acts 21:9*

UNSAFE PASSAGE
Unsuitable for Student-Led Prayer

Or don't you know that he who is joined to a **prostitute** is one body? For, "The two," says he, "will become one flesh." *1 Corinthians 6:16*

And he broke down the pavilions of the male **prostitutes** of the temple, that were in the house of the Lord, where the women wove hangings for the Asherah pole. *2 Kings 23:7*

The multitude of the **prostitution** of the alluring prostitute. *Nahum 3:4*

But **prove** all things. Hold fast that which is good. *1 Thessalonians 5:21*

Your head is like Carmel, and the hair of your head is like **purple**. *Song of Songs 7:5*

And it came to pass as we were going to prayer that a certain female slave, having a spirit of **Python**, met us. *Acts 16:16*

Q is for Qoph. I have called with my whole heart. *Psalms 119:145*

Peter was below in the **quadrangle**. *Mark 14:66*

Delivered him to four **quaternions** of soldiers to keep him. *Acts 12:4*

Come ye, I take wine, and we drink, **quaff** strong drink, and as this day hath been tomorrow, great—exceeding abundant! *Isaiah 56:12*

They asked, and he brought **quails**. *Psalms 105:40*

They were afraid of being driven on the Syrtis **quicksands**. They lowered the gear and lay to. *Acts 27:17*

R is for **Ragau**, which was the son of Phalec. *Luke 3:35*

Only **Rahab** the prostitute shall live. *Joshua 6:17*

A certain man of **Ramathaimzophim**. *1 Samuel 1:1*

Benjamin is a wolf that **raveneth**. *Genesis 49:27*

These are murmurers, **repiners**, according to their desires walking. *Jude 1:16*

Reprobate silver shall men call them. *Jeremiah 6:30*

Have you knowledge of **rock-goats**? Or do you see the roes giving birth? *Job 39:1*

Clothed with a cloud. A **rainbow** was on his head. *Revelation 10:1*

Strengthen me with **raisins**. *Song of Songs 2:5*

THE UNTOLD STORY
The Deleted Details from Popular Passages

Christ Jesus, who, subsisting in the form of God, did not esteem it an object of **rapine** to be on an equality with God. *Philippians 2:5-6*

She sat beside the reapers, and he **reached** her parched corn, and she did eat and was sufficed. *Ruth 2:14*

Refresh my bowels in the Lord. *Philemon 1:20*

On the seventh day you shall rest, that your ox and your donkey may have rest, and the son of your handmaid, and the alien may be **refreshed**. *Exodus 23:12*

The Lord will **rejoice** over you to destroy you. *Deuteronomy 28:63*

But **religion** is of profit in every way. *1 Timothy 4:8*

Naked I came out of my mother's womb, and naked shall I **return** there. *Job 1:21*

Canst thou bind the **rhinoceros** with thy thong to plough? *Job 39:10*

That great city, in which there are more than a hundred and twenty thousand persons that know not how to distinguish between their **right** hand and their left? *Jonah 4:11*

Then Elijah took off his **robe**, and, rolling it up, gave the water a blow with it, and the waters were parted. *2 Kings 2:8*

For their **rock** is not as our **rock**. *Deuteronomy 32:31*

S is for sackbut, psaltery, and all kinds of music. *Daniel 3:7*

At his table, my **spikenard** sendeth forth the smell thereof. *Song of Songs 1:12*

It bred worms and **stank**, and Moses was wroth with them. *Exodus 16:20*

The **stellio** supporteth itself on hands. *Proverbs 30:28*

And he revileth and **stoneth** with stones and hath dusted with dust. *2 Samuel 16:13*

Men of Babylon made **Succothbenoth**, and men of Cuth made Nergal. *2 Kings 17:30*

He that hateth **suretiship** is **sure**. *Proverbs 11:15*

PITY THE TRANSLATOR 8

Most people would not be surprised to learn that satyrs make few appearances in the Bible. Let's see how the King James Version dealt with Isaiah 13:21, followed by alternate interpretations.

" But **wild beasts** of the desert shall lie there, and their houses shall be full of **doleful creatures**, and **owls** shall dwell there, and **satyrs** shall dance there.

Wild beasts
King James

wild animals
World English Bible

Ziim
Young's Literal Translation

Doleful creatures
King James

crying jackals
Bible in Basic English

serpents
Douay-Rheims Bible

owls
Darby Bible Translation

jackals
World English Bible

howlings
Young's Literal Translation

Owls
King James

ostriches
American Standard Version

Satyrs
King James

wild goats
American Standard Version

evil spirits
Bible in Basic English

hairy ones
Douay-Rheims Bible

Let your talk be with grace, mixed with **salt**. *Colossians 4:6*

As for your birth, in the day you were born your navel was not cut, neither were you washed in water to cleanse you. You weren't **salted** at all. *Ezekiel 16:4*

Salt is good, but if the salt have lost its **saltness**, wherewith will ye season it? Have salt in yourselves. *Mark 9:50*

And he that sat was to look upon like a jasper and a **sardine stone**. *Revelation 4:3*

And the Lord said to the **Satan**, "See, I give all Job has into your hands, only do not put a finger on the man himself." And the Satan went out from before the Lord. *Job 1:12*

Surely he **scoffeth** at the **scoffers**. *Proverbs 3:34*

Her great **scum** went not forth out of her. Her **scum** shall be in the fire. *Ezekiel 24:12*

A wind from Yahweh went out and brought quails from the **sea**. *Numbers 11:31*

All the ships of the sea with their **seamen** were in you, trading in your goods. *Ezekiel 27:9*

Am I a sea or a **sea-monster**? *Job 7:12*

Praise Jehovah from the earth, ye **sea-monsters**. *Psalms 148:7*

The **sea-weeds** were twisted round my head. *Jonah 2:5*

Make their loins continually to **shake**. *Psalms 69:23*

And to those parts of the body which seem to have less honor we clothe with more honor. And to those parts of the body which are a cause of **shame** to us we give the greater respect. *1 Corinthians 12:23*

Issachar is a strong ass, couching down between the **sheepfolds**. *Genesis 49:14*

The mountains shall drop down new wine, and the hills shall flow with milk, and all the rivers of Judah shall flow with waters, and a fountain shall come forth out of the house of the Lord and shall water the valley of **Shittim**. *1 Samuel 19:10*

Do not let your foot be without **shoes**. *Jeremiah 2:25*

Also I **shook** my lap. *Nehemiah 5:13*

Take wheat, barley, beans, lentils, millet, and spelt, and put them in one vessel, and make bread. All the days when you shall lie on your **side**, 390 days, it will be your food. *Ezekiel 4:9*

And everything that she lieth upon in her separation shall be unclean. Everything also that she **sitteth** upon shall be unclean. *Leviticus 15:20*

Can the Ethiopian change his **skin**? *Jeremiah 13:23*

"Behold, I am against you," says Yahweh of Armies, "and I will lift your **skirts** over your face. I will show the nations your nakedness." *Nahum 3:5*

And they had brick for stone, and **slime** had they for mortar. *Genesis 11:3*

And bread of **sloth** she eateth not. *Proverbs 31:27*

If all the body was an eye, where would be the hearing? If all was hearing, where would be the **smelling**? *1 Corinthians 12:17*

There went up a **smoke** out of the Lord's nostrils and a devouring fire out of his mouth. *2 Samuel 22:9*

He turneth back and walketh in the house, once hither and once thither, and goeth up and stretcheth himself upon him, and the youth **sneezeth** till seven times. *2 Kings 4:35*

His **sneezings** flash forth light. *Job 41:18*

The glory of his **snorting** is awesome. *Job 39:20*

And he made his seven lamps, and his **snuffers**, and his **snuffdishes**, of pure gold. *Exodus 37:23*

For my people is foolish. They have not known me. They are **sottish** children. *Jeremiah 4:22*

He **speaketh** with his feet. *Proverbs 6:13*

Thus saith Jehovah of hosts, the God of Israel, "Drink ye, and be drunken, and **spew**, and fall, and rise no more." *Jeremiah 25:27*

Be like a gazelle or a young stag on the mountains of **spices**! *Song of Songs 8:14*

Let me alone till I swallow down my **spittle**? *Job 7:19*

Martha, the sister of him that was dead, saith to him, "Lord, by this time he **stinketh**, for he is now of four days." *John 11:39*

Dead flies cause the ointment of the apothecary to send forth a **stinking savour**. *Ecclesiastes 10:1*

The pollutions of the idols, and the whoredom, and the **strangled** thing, and the blood. *Acts 15:20*

And Moses **strippeth** Aaron of his garments. And Moses clotheth with them Eleazar his son, and Aaron dieth. *Numbers 20:28*

Then hath Jehovah made wonderful thy **strokes**, and the **strokes** of thy seed—great **strokes**. *Deuteronomy 28:59*

Thou shalt not wear a mingled **stuff**, wool and linen together. *Deuteronomy 22:11*

Of making many books there is no end, and much **study** is an affliction of the flesh. *Ecclesiastes 12:12*

Be not over just, and be not more wise than is necessary, lest thou become **stupid**. *Ecclesiastes 7:16*

And the Lord's anger was kindled the same time, and he **swore**. *Numbers 32:10*

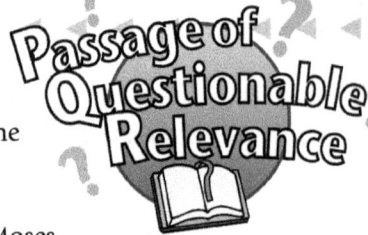

T is for *tabernacling* with them in the midst. *Leviticus 16:16*

Thou shalt make fifty **taches** of gold and couple the curtains. *Exodus 26:6*

And they turned **thitherward**. *Judges 18:15*

Be set free from the **thraldom**. *Romans 8:21*

And he smote **thrice** and stayed. *2 Kings 13:18*

Under a **tutor-slave**. *Galatians 3:25*

For the power of the horses is in their mouths and in their **tails**. For their **tails** are like serpents, and have heads, and with them they harm. *Revelation 9:19*

And Jonah said to them, "**Take** me and cast me into the sea." *Jonah 1:12*

Truly I say to you, that **tax-farmers** and loose women are going into the kingdom of God before you. *Matthew 21:31*

THE UNTOLD STORY
The Deleted Details from Popular Passages

TALKING ANIMALS
(and plants etc.) OF THE BIBLE

And the **serpent** said unto the woman, "Ye shall not surely die." —*Genesis 3:4*

And the **ass** said unto Balaam, "Am not I thine ass?" —*Numbers 22:30*

The **trees** said unto the olive tree, "Reign thou over us." —*Judges 9:8*

But the **olive tree** said unto them, "Should I leave my fatness?" —*Judges 9:9*

But the **fig tree** said unto them, "Should I forsake my sweetness?" —*Judges 9:11*

And the **vine** said unto them, "Should I leave my wine?" —*Judges 9:13*

And the **bramble** said unto the trees, "Put your trust in my shadow." —*Judges 9:15*

The **fish** of the sea shall declare to you. —*Job 12:8*

Do the **lightnings** report to you, "Here we are"? —*Job 38:35*

The **horseleach** hath two daughters, crying, "Give, give." —*Proverbs 30:15*

The **trees of Lebanon** saying, "No wood-cutter has come up against us with an axe." —*Isaiah 14:8*

The shouting of **mountains**. —*Ezekiel 7:7*

The voice of **pelican** and the **porcupine** shall sing. —*Zephaniah 2:14*

And the **four beasts** saying, "Holy, holy, holy." —*Revelation 4:7*

And **every creature** in heaven, on earth, and under the earth, and in the sea, heard I saying, "Blessing, and honor, and glory, and power." —*Revelation 5:13*

I heard an **eagle** saying with a loud voice, "Woe! Woe! Woe!" —*Revelation 8:13*

And there was given unto the **beast** a mouth speaking great things and blasphemies. —*Revelation 13:5*

Another beast had two horns like a lamb, and he spake as a dragon. —*Revelation 13:11*

And a fighter came out from the tents of the Philistines, named Goliath of Gath, who was **ten** feet tall. *1 Samuel 17:4*

And Michal took the **teraphim**, and laid it in the bed, and put a pillow of goats' hair at the head thereof, and covered it with the clothes. *1 Samuel 19:13*

Whom God went to redeem to be his own people, to make thee a name of greatness and **terribleness**. *1 Chronicles 17:21*

The sinews of his **testicles** are wrapped together. *Job 40:17*

My little finger shall be **thicker** than my father's loins. *1 Kings 12:10*

O prince's daughter! The roundings of thy **thighs** are like jewels. *Song of Songs 7:1*

Thus saith the Lord, "There is an accursed **thing** in the midst of thee. And it shall be that he that is taken with the accursed thing shall be burnt with fire, he and all that he hath." And Joshua, and all Israel with him, took Achan, and all Israel stoned him with stones, and burned them with fire, after they had stoned them with stones. *Joshua 7:13,15,24,25*

And Gideon made an ephod of it and put it in his city in Ophrah, and all Israel went **thither** a whoring after it. *Judges 8:27*

And in order to make the house clean, let him take two birds and cedar wood and red **thread**. *Leviticus 14:49*

Put a knife to your **throat**, if you are a man given to appetite. *Proverbs 23:2*

He makes **thunder-flames** for the rain. He sends out the winds from his store-houses. *Psalms 135:7*

The daughters of Zion are haughty and walk with stretched forth necks and wanton eyes, walking and mincing as they go and making a **tinkling** with their feet. *Isaiah 3:16*

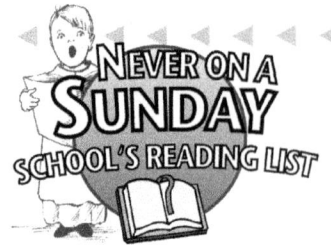

Will a man rob God? But ye say, "Wherein have we robbed thee?" In **tithes** and offerings. *Malachi 3:8*

He killed it, and Moses took some of its blood and put it on the tip of Aaron's right ear, and on the thumb of his right hand, and on the great **toe** of his right foot. *Leviticus 8:23*

And Jesus took him aside from the multitude, and put his fingers into his ears, and he spit, and touched his **tongue**. *Mark 7:33*

When the king of Israel had read the letter, he **tore** his clothes. *2 Kings 5:7*

Neither let the eunuch say, "Behold, I am a dry **tree**." *Isaiah 56:3*

U is for *Ucal*. Truly I am more stupid than anyone. *Proverbs 30:1-2*

Won't his **uncircumcision** be accounted as circumcision? *Romans 2:26*

I save you from all your **uncleannesses**, and I will call for the corn. *Ezekiel 36:29*

And digged an **under-winevat**. *Mark 12:1*

Yet being **unperfect**. *Psalms 139:16*

I am merciful to their **unrighteousnesses**. *Hebrews 8:12*

Two or three **unsexed** servants put out their heads. *2 Kings 9:32*

And heard **unutterable** sayings. *2 Corinthians 12:4*

Thighs girt with gold of **Uphaz**. *Daniel 10:5*

Uz his firstborn, Buz his brother. *Genesis 22:21*

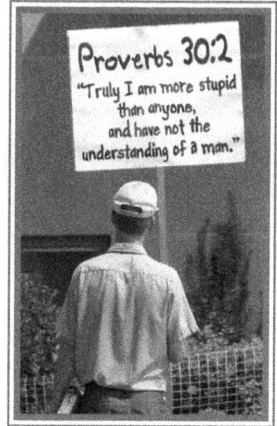

> Proverbs 30:2
> "Truly I am more stupid than anyone, and have not the understanding of a man."

"I believe. Help my **unbelief**!" *Mark 9:24*

My servant Isaiah has gone **unclothed** and without shoes for three years. *Isaiah 20:3*

But if any man think that he behaveth himself **uncomely** toward his virgin, if she pass the flower of her age and need so require, let him do what he will. *1 Corinthians 7:36*

His **underparts** are like sharp potsherds. He spreadeth as it were a threshing wain upon the mire. *Job 41:30*

To convict all the **ungodly** of them of all their works of **ungodliness**, which they have wrought **ungodlily**. *Jude 1:15*

God brought them out of Egypt. He hath as it were the strength of a **unicorn**. *Numbers 23:22*

HIDDEN BIBLE
BAND NAMES 5

King David famously plays an ancient style of harp, but another style of music is suggested in Job 28:9: "Man puts out his hand on the **hard rock**."

Tabernacles of the Perverse *–Job 18:21*

There Shall Be Stink *–Isaiah 3:24*

They Become Monsters *–Exodus 7:12*

Thrust Me *–1 Samuel 31:4*

The Unicorn with his Band *–Job 39:10*

Utter Things *–Matthew 13:35*

Very Naughty Figs *–Jeremiah 24:2*

Wealth Profiteth *–Proverbs 11:4*

Unnatural Vice *–Jude 1:7*

The Valley of Ono *–Nehemiah 6:2*

NEVER ON A SUNDAY SCHOOL'S READING LIST

Let the marriage bed be **unpolluted**. *Hebrews 13:4*

Why do thy disciples eat bread with **unwashen** hands? *Mark 7:5*

That Jehovah may do his work, his strange work, and perform his act, his **unwonted** act. *Isaiah 28:21*

He didn't leave him a single one who **urinates** on a wall. *1 Kings 16:11*

And God said, "Let **us** make man in our image, like **us**." *Genesis 1:26*

The table, and its staves, and all its **utensils**, and the shewbread. *Exodus 35:13*

Be **utter** babes. *1 Corinthians 14:20*

V is for **Vajezatha** the ten sons of Haman. *Esther 9:9-10*

Vedan and Javan traded with yarn. *Ezekiel 27:19*

To see the **verdure**. *Song of Songs 6:11*

They were numbered and **victualled**, and they went against them. *1 Kings 20:27*

He who is weak eats only **vegetables**. *Romans 14:2*

Whoso is eating their eggs doth die, and the crushed egg becomes a **viper**. *Isaiah 59:5*

Wherever the dead body is, there will the **vultures** flock together. *Matthew 24:28*

W is for **water-skin**, and put the boy on her back. *Genesis 21:14*

Waw. And meet me doth thy kindness. *Psalms 119:41*

They did work **wilily** and made as if they had been ambassadors. *Joshua 9:4*

The mantles, and the **wimples**, and the crisping pins. *Isaiah 3:22*

Seven green **withs**, which had not been dried. *Judges 16:8*

Smite the loins of his **withstanders**. *Deuteronomy 33:11*

Behold, my master **wotteth** not what is with me in the house. *Genesis 39:8*

Then he took his eldest son that should have reigned in his stead and offered him for a burnt offering upon the **wall**. *2 Kings 3:27*

If the plague is greenish or reddish in the garment, or in the skin, or in the **warp**, or in the **woof**, or in anything made of skin, it is the plague of leprosy. *Leviticus 13:49*

Blind, injured, maimed, having a **wart**, festering, or having a running sore, you shall not offer them to Yahweh. *Leviticus 22:22*

The beginning of strife is as when one letteth out **water**. *Proverbs 17:14*

Ye shall bring out of your habitations two **wave** loaves of two tenth deals. *Leviticus 23:17*

The heave-thigh and the **wave-breast** shall they bring. *Leviticus 10:15*

And he that hath clean hands shall **wax** stronger and stronger. *Job 17:9*

As for the wheels, it was cried unto them in my hearing, "O **wheel**." *Ezekiel 10:13*

Their whole body, their backs, their hands, their wings, and the wheels, were full of eyes round about, even the **wheels**. *Ezekiel 10:12*

Yahweh said to Satan, "**Where** have you come from?" *Job 1:7*

There appeared a chariot of fire and horses of fire, and parted them both asunder, and Elijah went up by a **whirlwind** into heaven. *2 Kings 2:11*

 Bible Funmentionables' Basic Bible Math

UNEQUIVOCAL EQUIVALENCIES

Translations vary widely. In Proverbs 30:28 the Hebrew word "תִּמָמ" has been translated as "spider" and also as "lizard." Therefore, biblically speaking, a spider equals a lizard. Follow along as we recklessly apply this logic using the transitive property (if a=b, and b=c, then a=c).

If a **spider** = a **lizard**
King James   Prov. 30:28   English Revised Version

and a **lizard** = a **tortoise**
Darby   Lev. 11:29   King James

THEN a **spider** = a **tortoise**

And by substituting tortoise for spider we reach the following decidedly unorthodox variation on Isaiah 59:5:

Eggs of a viper they have hatched, and webs of a *tortoise* they weave.

If a **slug** = a **snail**
New International Version   Psa. 58:8   King James

and a **snail** = a **lizard**
King James   Lev. 11:30   Douay-Rheims

and a **lizard** = a **crocodile**
Darby   Lev. 11:29   Douay-Rheims

and a **crocodile** = a **whale**
GOD'S WORD® Translation   Eze. 32:2   King James

and a **whale** = a **sea monster**
King James   Matt. 12:40   Weymouth

THEN a **slug** = a **sea monster**

And by this logic, Matthew 12:40 becomes

For as Jonah was three days in the *slug*'s belly, so will the Son of Man be three days in the heart of the earth.

If a **weasel** = a **mole**
King James   Lev. 11:29   Darby

and a **mole** = a **chameleon**
King James   Lev.11:30   Bible in Basic English

and a **chameleon** = a **crocodile**
King James   Lev. 11:30   New American Standard

and a **crocodile** = a **dragon**
GOD'S WORD® Translation   Eze. 32:2   Douay-Rheims

and a **dragon** = a **leviathan**
Douay-Rheims   Psa. 74:14   King James

THEN a **weasel** = a **leviathan**

So now you know what a leviathan is. By substitution, we now have the new and improved Job 41:22:

There is strength in *weasel*'s neck. Terror dances before him.

Blessed is he **who watches** and keeps his clothes, so that he doesn't walk naked, and they see his shame. *Revelation 16:15*

▷ But if her husband dies, she is at liberty to marry **whom** she **will**, provided that he is a Christian. *1 Corinthians 7:39*

For a **whore** is a deep ditch, and a strange woman is a narrow pit. *Proverbs 23:27*

And because of the **whoredom**, let each man have his own wife. *1 Corinthians 7:2*

UNSAFE PASSAGE

Unsuitable for Student-Led Prayer

▷ ▷ For by means of a **whorish woman** a man is brought to a piece of bread. *Proverbs 6:26* ◁

Their inward part is very **wickedness**. Their throat is an open sepulchre. *Psalms 5:9*

David came to his house at Jerusalem, and the king took the ten women his concubines, whom he had left to keep the house, and put them in custody, and provided them with sustenance, but didn't go in to them. So they were shut up to the day of their death, living in **widowhood**. *2 Samuel 20:3*

And Caleb said, "He that smiteth Kirjathsepher, and taketh it, to him will I give Achsah my daughter to **wife**." And Othniel, Caleb's nephew, took it, and he gave Othniel his daughter to wife. *Judges 1:12-13*

SPOKEN-TO ANIMALS
(and plants etc.)
OF THE BIBLE

Or speak to **the earth**. –*Job 12:8*

And the Lord spoke to the **fish** and it vomited out Jonah upon the dry land. –*Jonah 2:10*

If ye shall say unto this **mountain**, "Be thou removed." –*Matthew 21:21*

And Jesus said unto the **fig tree**, "No man eat fruit of thee hereafter forever." –*Mark 11:14*

Whosoever shall say unto this **mountain**, "Be thou removed." –*Mark 11:23*

Command this **black-mulberry-tree**, "Tear up your roots and plant yourself in the sea," and instantly it would. –*Luke 17:6*

And I saw an angel saying to all the **birds** that fly in mid-heaven, "Come, gather yourselves." –*Revelation 19:17*

A vain man is bold, and the colt of a **wild** ass man is born. *Job 11:12*

For where a last **will** and testament is, there must of necessity be the death of him who made it. *Hebrews 9:16*

Make me strong with **wine-cakes**, let me be comforted with apples. I am overcome with love. *Song of Songs 2:5*

Wherefore art thou red in thine apparel, and thy garments like him that treadeth in the **winefat**? *Isaiah 63:2*

▷ The **wing** of the ostrich rejoiceth. *Job 39:13*

Neither let those who hate me without a cause **wink** their eyes. *Psalms 35:19*

And the times of this ignorance God **winked** at. *Acts 17:30*

I will **wipe** Jerusalem as a man wipeth a dish, wiping it, and turning it upside down. *2 Kings 21:13*

Who numbereth the clouds with **wisdom**? Or who poureth out the bottles of the heavens? *Job 38:37*

So that they go around naked **without** clothing. *Job 24:10*

And Gideon had threescore and ten sons of his body begotten, for he had many **wives**. *Judges 8:30*

For their **worm** shall not die. *Isaiah 66:24*

And with the perverse thou shewest thyself a **wrestler**. *2 Samuel 22:27*

X is for *Xanthicus* on the 30th day with security. *2 Maccabees 11:30*

Now when every virgin's turn came to go in to King **Xerxes**, after all had been done for setting them off to advantage, it was the twelfth month, so that for six months they were anointed with oil of myrrh. *Esther 2:12*

Y is for *Yah*, *Yah* in the land of the living. *Isaiah 38:11*

Moses gave it the name **Yahweh-nissi**. *Exodus 17:15*

Yod. Thy hands made me. *Psalms 119:73*

Do not make false decisions in questions of **yardsticks**. *Leviticus 19:35*

He didn't tell them to beware of the **yeast** of bread. *Matthew 16:12*

If the itch has spread in the skin, the priest shall not look for the **yellow** hair. *Leviticus 13:36*

Crushing the head of the poor, and turning the steps of the gentle out of the way, and a man and his father go in unto the same **young** woman. *Amos 2:7*

Passage of Questionable Relevance

Both young men and maidens, old men with **youths**. *Psalms 148:12*

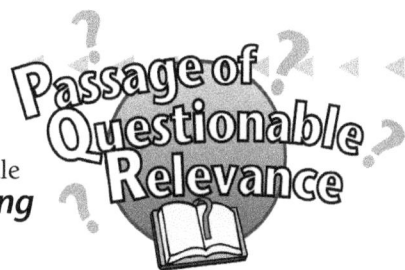

Z is for *Zaanannim*, which is by Kedesh. *Judges 4:11*

Ammonites call them **Zamzummim**. *Deuteronomy 2:20*

Pharaoh called Joseph **Zaphnathpaaneah** and gave him to wife. *Genesis 41:45*

Go, inquire of Baal **Zebub**, the god of Ekron. *2 Kings 1:2*

Nobles like Oreb and **Zeeb**, their princes like **Zebah** and **Zalmunna**. *Psalms 83:11*

In the month **Ziv**, which is the second month. *1 Kings 6:1*

By the ascent of **Ziz**, and you shall find them. *2 Chronicles 20:16*

His disciples remembered that it was written, "**Zeal** for your house will eat me up." *John 2:17*

For Jehovah, whose name is **Zealous**, is a **zealous** God. *Exodus 34:14*

The daughters of **Zelophehad** were married to their father's brothers' sons. *Numbers 36:11*

Therefore dwell do **Ziim** with Iim. *Jeremiah 50:39*

When all the peoples heard the sound of the horn, flute, **zither**, lyre, harp, pipe, and all kinds of music, all the peoples, the nations, and the languages, fell down. *Daniel 3:7*

When they were come to the land of **Zuph**, Saul said to his servant that was with him, "Come and let us return, lest my father stop caring for the asses." *1 Samuel 9:5*

THE END of Tamar? Then Judah said to Tamar, his daughter-in-law, "Remain a widow in your father's house, until my son *Shelah becomes a man.*" Tamar took off of her the garments of her widowhood, and covered herself with her veil, and sat in the gate of Enaim, for she saw that Shelah was now a man, but she had not been made his wife. When Judah saw her, he thought that she was a prostitute, for she had covered her face. He turned to her and said, "Please let me come in to you," for he didn't know that she was his daughter-in-law. About three months later, Judah was told, "Tamar is with child by prostitution." Judah said, "Bring her forth, and *let her be burnt.*" When she was brought forth, she sent to her father-in-law, saying, "By Judah, I am with child." Judah said, "*She is more righteous than I, because I didn't give her to Shelah, my son.*" *Excerpts from Genesis 38:11,14-16,24-26*

THE END of Lot's Wife (who for some reason has no name) Then the Lord rained upon Sodom and Gomorrah brimstone and fire out of heaven. But Lot's wife looked back from behind him, and she became *a pillar of salt.* *Excerpts from Genesis 19:24,26*

THE END of Isaac? God put Abraham to the test, and said unto him, "Abraham, take now thy dearly loved only son Isaac, and *offer him for a burnt offering* upon one of the mountains which I will tell thee of." And they came to the place which God had told him of, and Abraham built the altar there, and laid the wood in order, and bound Isaac his son, and laid him on the altar upon the wood. And Abraham stretched forth his hand, and took the knife to slay his son, and the angel of the Lord called unto him out of heaven, and said, "Abraham, lay not thine hand upon the lad, for now I know that thou fearest God. *Because thou hast done this thing, I will bless thee*, and I will multiply thy seed as the stars of the heaven, and thy seed shall possess the gate of his enemies."

Excerpts from Genesis 22:1,2,9-12,16-17

THE END of the Smiting Egyptian Moses spied an Egyptian smiting a Hebrew brethren. And *he looked this way and that way*, and when he saw that there was no man, he slew the Egyptian, and hid him in the sand. *Excerpts from Exodus 2:11-12*

THE END of Nadab and Abihu And Nadab and Abihu died before the Lord, when *they offered strange fire* before the Lord in the wilderness of Sinai. *Excerpts from Numbers 3:4*

THE END of Korah and Company and the Perfume Men And they assembled against Moses and Aaron, and said unto them, "Enough of you!" And Moses said, "If the Lord does something new, opening the earth to take them in, then it will be clear to you that the Lord has not been honored by these men." And while these words were on his lips, the earth under them was parted in two. And *the earth, opening her mouth, took them in*, with their families. So they went down living into the underworld, and the earth was shut over them. Then fire came out from the Lord, burning up the 250 men who were offering the perfume. *Excerpts from Number 16:3,28,30-33,35*

THE END of Baalpeor's Followers So *Israel had relations with the women of Moab in honor of Baalpeor*, and the Lord was moved to wrath against Israel. And the Lord said unto Moses, "Take all the heads of the people and hang them up before the Lord against the sun, that the fierce anger of the Lord may be turned away from Israel." *Numbers 25:3-4*

THE END of the Midianitish Woman and Her Man And, behold, one of the children of Israel came and brought unto his brethren *a Midianitish woman* in the sight of Moses. And when Phinehas saw it, he rose up from among the congregation, and *took a javelin in his hand,* and he went after the man of Israel into the tent, and thrust both of them through, the man of Israel, and the woman through her belly. So the plague was stayed from the children of Israel. *Excerpts from Numbers 25:6-8*

THE END of Sisera Then Jael, Heber's wife, took a tent-pin and a hammer and went up to Sisera quietly, *driving the pin into his head*, and it went through his head into the earth, for he was in *a deep sleep* from weariness. And so he came to his end. *Judges 4:21*

THE END of Uzzah Uzzah put forth his hand to the ark of God, and took hold of it, for the oxen shook it. And the anger of the Lord was kindled against Uzzah, and *God smote him there for his error.* And there he died by the ark of God. *Excerpts from 2 Samuel 6:6-7*

THE END of Absalom And Absalom rode upon a mule, and the mule went under the thick boughs of a great oak, and *his head caught hold of the oak*, and he was taken up between the heaven and the earth. And the mule that was under him went away. Then Joab took three darts in his hand, and thrust them through the heart of Absalom, while he was yet alive in the midst of the oak. *Excerpts from 2 Samuel 18:9,14*

THE END of Amasa And Joab took Amasa by the beard with the right hand to kiss him. But Amasa took no heed to the sword that was in Joab's hand. So he smote him therewith in the fifth rib and *shed out his bowels to the ground*, and he died. *Excerpts from 2 Samuel 20:9-10*

THE END of Sheba "Sheba the son of Bichri hath lifted up his hand against the king, even against David. Deliver him only, and I will depart from the city." And the woman said unto Joab, "Behold, *his head shall be thrown to thee over the wall.*" Then the woman went unto all the people in her wisdom. And they cut off the head of Sheba the son of Bichri and cast it out to Joab. *Excerpts from 2 Samuel 20:21-22*

AN END IS COME,

THE END IS COME ...

— *Ezekiel 7:6*

THE END of 450 of Baal's Prophets Elijah came near to all the people, and said, "How long will you waver between the two sides? If Yahweh is God, follow him, but if Baal, then follow him. You call on the name of your gods, and I will call on the name of Yahweh, and the God that answereth by fire, *let him be God.*" And they called on the name of Baal, but there was no voice that answered. Then the fire of Yahweh fell and consumed the burnt-sacrifice, the wood, the stones, and the dust. And Elijah said to them, "Take the prophets of Baal." And they took the prophets of Baal and slew them there. *Excerpts from 1 Kings 18:21,24,26,38,40*

THE END of the Asherah Pole And King Josiah brought out the Asherah pole from the house of Yahweh, outside of Jerusalem, to the brook Kidron, and burned it, and beat it to dust, and *cast its dust on the graves of the common people.* *2 Kings 23:6*

THE END of Job's Family, Servants, Livestock, and Home A messenger to Job said, "The oxen were plowing, and the donkeys feeding beside them, and the Sabeans attacked and took them away. *The fire of God has fallen from the sky* and has burned up the sheep and the servants. The Chaldeans swept down on the camels and have taken them away. Your sons and your daughters were eating and drinking wine in their eldest brother's house, and behold, there came a great wind from the wilderness, and struck the four corners of the house, and it fell on the young men, and they are dead." Then Job arose, and tore his robe, and shaved his head. *Excerpts from Job 1:14-20*

THE END of Samaria's Idols All of Samaria's idols will be beaten to pieces, and all her temple gifts will be burned with fire, and all her images I will destroy, for she has gathered these things from *the fee of her prostitution*, and to the fee of prostitution shall they return. *Micah 1:7*

THE END of Ananias A certain man named Ananias, with Saphira his wife, sold a piece of land, and by fraud *kept back part of the price of the land.* And bringing a certain part of it, laid it at the feet of the apostles. But Peter said, "Ananias, why hath Satan tempted thy heart, that thou shouldst lie to the Holy Ghost, and by fraud keep part of the price of the land? Thou hast not lied to men, but to God." And Ananias hearing these words, fell down, and gave up the ghost. *Excerpts from Acts 5:1-6*

INDEX

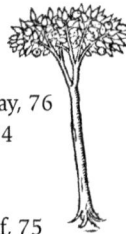

www.ingramcontent.com/pod-product-compliance
Lightning Source LLC
Chambersburg PA
CBHW062102090426
42741CB00015B/3310